The Epistle of the Apostle Paul to The
ROMANS

Register This New Book

Benefits of Registering*

- ✓ FREE **replacements** of lost or damaged books
- ✓ FREE **audiobook** – *Pilgrim's Progress*, audiobook edition
- ✓ FREE information about new titles and other **freebies**

www.anekopress.com/new-book-registration

*See our website for requirements and limitations.

The Epistle of the Apostle Paul to The
ROMANS

A COMMENTARY

J. MARTIN

We love hearing from our readers. Please contact us at www.anekopress.com/questions-comments with any questions, comments, or suggestions.

Romans: A Commentary – J. Martin
Copyright © 2018
First edition published 2018

All rights reserved. No part of this book may be reproduced, stored in a retrieval system, or transmitted in any form or by any means – electronic, mechanical, photocopying, recording, or otherwise, without written permission from the publisher.

Scripture quotations are taken from the Jubilee Bible, copyright © 2000, 2001, 2010, 2013 by Russell M. Stendal. Used by permission of Russell M. Stendal, Bogota, Colombia. All rights reserved.

Cover Design: J. Martin
Cover Images: Nik Merkulov/Shutterstock & LUMIKK555/Shutterstock

Aneko Press
www.anekopress.com
Aneko Press, Life Sentence Publishing, and our logos are trademarks of
Life Sentence Publishing, Inc.
203 E. Birch Street
P.O. Box 652
Abbotsford, WI 54405

RELIGION / Biblical Commentary / New Testament / Paul's Letters

Paperback ISBN: 978-1-62245-607-9

eBook ISBN: 978-1-62245-608-6

10   9   8   7   6   5   4   3   2

Available where books are sold

Contents

Introduction vii

Romans 1 1

Romans 2 11

Romans 3 19

Romans 4 27

Romans 5 35

Romans 6 41

Romans 7 49

Romans 8 57

Romans 9 69

Romans 10 81

Romans 11 89

Romans 12 99

Romans 13 107

Romans 14 111

Romans 15 117

Romans 16 127

Other Books to Enjoy 133

Introduction

It is my sincerest desire is to point people back to the scriptures for all answers. This isn't as much as commentary, then, as it is an attempt to revitalize interest in the scriptures themselves. My prayer is that this endeavor does exactly that. May the Lord bless you.

– J. Martin

Romans 1

1 ¶ Paul, slave of Jesus, the Christ, called *to be* an apostle, separated unto the gospel of God

> Paul was certainly and unmistakable *called to be an apostle* while on the road to Damascus. Our God is not mute and if He has something for us to do, we may know for certain that it is Him calling us to the work. This is not to cast doubt on whether or not we should be an active Christian, but to say that we needn't worry about our specific and individual calling – God will certainly reveal our calling to us, if we have sincere hearts for the Lord and in sincerity wait on Him for direction. And then as Paul responded, when He has called us, we must respond in ready obedience to the call.

2 (which he had promised before by his prophets in the holy scriptures)

3 of his Son (who was born unto him of the seed of David according to the flesh,

Without a moment's delay, Paul makes sure his readers know that this is about Jesus Christ, not about Paul. In verse 1 he says he is a *slave* of Jesus Christ, and what he's *called* to is the Gospel of Jesus Christ. In verses 2 and 3, he makes it clear that this is not a new Jesus or a false gospel, but the same Jesus Christ the prophets prophesied of. If we genuinely know and love the Lord, our whole desire and motivation will be to declare Jesus Christ, while simultaneously making it clear that we are merely the Lord's slaves (v. 1).

4 who was declared *to be* the Son of God with power, according to the Spirit of sanctification, by the resurrection from the dead), of Jesus, the Christ, our Lord.

If Jesus had died on the cross but not risen from the dead, He might have been dismissed as a false prophet (as the Jewish leaders also knew, and through their attempt to conceal the resurrection [Matthew 18:11-25], hoped to convince others that Jesus wasn't the Christ). But Jesus *did not* stay in the tomb. He really did rise on the third day and fulfilled prophecy to demonstrate that He was who He said He was – the Son of God and the Savior of all who believe.

5 By whom we have received the grace and the apostleship, to *cause* the faith to be obeyed among all the Gentiles in his name,

6 among whom ye are also the called of Jesus Christ;

"By whom" (v. 5) shows that Paul received "the grace and the apostleship" from Jesus Christ. Not from other men, and certainly not from Paul himself. V. 6 makes it clear that the same is true for those Paul is writing to; Paul is not calling men to Christ – it is Jesus Christ Himself who is calling men to Himself. Even though the message was being delivered through Paul, it was still Jesus Christ's message and His calling, not Paul's.

7 to all that are in Rome, beloved of God, called *to be* saints; ye have grace and peace of God our Father and of the Lord Jesus, the Christ.

We are "called to be saints," a very high calling. Within our natural selves, we have no desire to be saints, rather preferring to blend with the world in our speech, activities, and employment. But to be a saint means to truly deny ourselves and follow our Lord and Savior, Jesus Christ.

8 ¶ First, I thank my God through Jesus, the Christ, regarding you all, that your faith is preached in all the world.

The whole world knew that Romans were coming to Christ, this created no small stir. Our family, our friends, and our neighbors should likewise know about our faith, and if the church in any country of the world experienced the conversion as the Romans experienced, it could be anticipated that the whole world would be watching. Genuine revival needs no advertising.

9 For God is my witness, whom I serve in my spirit in the gospel of his Son, that without ceasing I always remember you in my prayers,

> Here is a lesson on prayer. Does this mean we should constantly be breathing prayers up to heaven as we go about our day, an unspoken thought directed to heaven as we work? Even a little searching in scripture will make it clear that this shallow type of prayer is not biblical. "Without ceasing" here is simply indicates that Paul prayed for the Romans regularly, without giving up. It doesn't not mean that Paul was literally praying all the time, even while about the other duties of the day. All scripture indicates that when men prayed, they stopped all other activities and prayed sincerely and reverently, with all attention directed towards the Lord while in prayer.

10 making request, if by any means now at length I might have a prosperous journey by the will of God to come unto you.

11 For I long to see you that I may impart with you some spiritual gift to confirm you,

12 that is, that I may be comforted together with you by the mutual faith both of you and me.

> Notice that Paul did not want to visit the Romans in order to help them restructure their denomination or to discuss more effective methods of ministry, but to impart "some spiritual gift." This concept of

imparting spiritual gifts is unfortunately lacking in most of the church, though in some churches the gifts are sought in extrabiblical ways. But the genuine is what we need, and if we want to be comforted that our ministry is of the Lord, seeing others receive spiritual gifts imparted by us is such a confirmation.

13 Now I would not have you ignorant, brethren, that many times I purposed to come unto you (but up until now I have been unable) that I might have some fruit among you also, even as among other Gentiles.

14 I am debtor both to the Greeks and to the Barbarians; both to the wise and to the unwise.

15 So, as much as in me is, I am ready to announce the gospel to you that are at Rome also.

16 ¶ For I am not ashamed of the gospel of the Christ; for it is *the* power of God *to give* saving health to every one that believes: to the Jew first and also to the Greek.

> "For I am not ashamed of the gospel of the Christ." These are convicting words. Am I ashamed of the gospel of Jesus Christ? Much of the church today is overly careful in how the gospel is presented lest people become offended, but isn't this often just us being ashamed of the gospel of Jesus Christ? This gospel is not necessarily offensive, but redeeming. It is not necessarily condemning, but freeing. If we genuinely love the Lord and understand the power of the gospel, we ought not to worry about those who will become offended, but make sure we are

handling the gospel with all reverence and diligence and truthfulness.

17 For in him is the righteousness of God revealed from faith to faith, as it is written, The just shall live by faith.

18 For the wrath of God is revealed from heaven against all ungodliness and injustice of men, who hold back the truth with injustice;

> *Therefore sin is still in the one that knows to do good and does not do it.* The same is true if we know the truth, and hold it back (v. 18). If God cares for the truth to be made known, He will also equip the saints to share the truth boldly and clearly.
>
> Whatever the biblical truth is that is being withheld, one cannot expect to get away lightly. The truth must be revealed to the world, for their salvation or their damnation (Mark 16:16), and for teaching and exhortation (2 Timothy 4:2).

19 ¶ because that which is known of God is manifest to them; for God has showed *it* unto them.

20 For the invisible things of him, his eternal power and divinity, are clearly understood by the creation of the world and by the things that are made so that there is no excuse;

> The creation of the world and all that is in it is clear evidence of God. When we sit down to eat a dinner, it is obvious that someone cooked the food; and because it looks good and tastes good, we know that

cook was talented and careful in all his preparations and making of the meal. As we go about our duties, we can easily see the evidence of a creator, and there is no excuse for not believing (v. 20). The human body itself is an amazing creation, and if one examines any one component of our physical bodies, he cannot help but be in awe. For example, who can comprehend how a brain analyzes, stores, and retrieves information? While it is true that today's supercomputers are capable of storing vast amounts of information and processing complicated calculations, the reality is that they were designed using the human brains God created and even then, today's supercomputers pale when compared to how our brain functions. Nothing exists without that same original Creator, and everything pales when compared to His fantastic creation. There truly is no excuse for unbelievers.

21 because having known God, they did not glorify *him* as God, neither were thankful, but became vain in their imaginations, and their foolish heart was darkened.

22 Professing themselves to be wise, they became fools

23 and exchanged the glory of the incorruptible God for *the* likeness of *an* image of corruptible man and of birds and of fourfooted beasts and of serpents.

While we don't see much idol worship in the western world (v. 23), it is clear that most of society doesn't glorify God, neither are they thankful to Him (v. 21). While America was founded on biblical principles, now we are "professing ourselves as wise, but became fools" and neither are we thankful, but are become vain in our imaginations (v. 21).

24 Therefore God also gave them over to the lusts of their own hearts for uncleanness, to contaminate their own bodies between *themselves*,

> This sounds a lot like the rampant sexual perversion seen everywhere today, does it not? Not only are individuals "contaminating their own bodies between themselves," they are even encouraged to do so by the leaders of our governments, organizations, and communities. This is resulting in an accelerating, downward spiral.

25 who changed the truth of God into a lie and worshipped and served the creature rather than the Creator, who is blessed for all ages. Amen.

26 For this cause God gave them up unto shameful affections, for even their women changed the natural use into that which is against nature;

27 and likewise also the males, leaving the natural use of the females, burned in their lust one toward another, males with males committing nefarious works and receiving in themselves the recompense that proceeded from their error.

> Paul does not address homosexuality as a "struggle," or as a result of something bad that happened because of our childhood. Instead, he addresses the reality of why these things are taking place – because

society as a whole is no longer worshipping God. Does this negate the individuals' responsibility in gross sin? Not at all.

28 And even as they did not like to retain God in *their* knowledge, God gave them over to a perverse understanding, to do those things which are not convenient,

> Forget God, and the below list of evil (v. 29-31) will soon follow. The world today is saying that we should be able to do whatever we want to be and be whoever we want to be. There are always consequences for our outward and inward sins though, we cannot avoid it. Law enforcement officers and anyone tasked with keeping order in society is to be pitied. They are fighting a losing battle as leaders encourage people to "explore who they are" while at the same time expecting peace in our land. Good and evil cannot and will not mix. If we as a society encourage evil, we will suffer the consequences as a whole.

29 being filled with all unrighteousness, fornication, wickedness, covetousness, maliciousness; full of envy, murder, debate, deceit, malignity; whisperers,

30 backbiters, haters of God, despiteful, proud, boasters, inventors of evil things, disobedient to parents,

31 without understanding, covenant breakers, without natural affection, implacable, without mercy.

32 Who having understood the righteousness of God, they did not understand that those who do such things are worthy of death, not only those that do the same, but even those who encourage those that do them.

If we trample the mercy of God underfoot (Hebrews 10:29), we are worthy of death (v. 32). But it doesn't stop there – if we encourage others to sin (v. 32) we are also worthy of death. How much do Christians laugh at perversion, how often we wink at fornication or other sins? How easily we make light of what God clearly calls sin. Beware of the consequences of all sin, even the sin of encouraging others to sin.

Romans 2

1 ⁋ Therefore, thou art inexcusable, O man, whosoever thou art that judgest; for in that which thou dost judge another, thou dost condemn thyself; for thou that judgest *others* doest the same things.

This verse is often mistakenly used to teach that we should not judge others, and in addition, that we are as much a sinner as the one we judge. This is a twisted understanding of this passage, and while there is some aspect of truth to it, that is not what Paul is saying here.

What Paul is saying in this verse that we are inexcusable for our own sins if we are capable of seeing the sins in others. There is no longer an excuse for our sin, if our eyes are open to seeing it in others. This verse is not about not judging others, but about us making sure we do not sin ourselves. This is confirmed by the following verses in this chapter.

2 For we are sure that the judgment of God is according to *the* truth against those who do such things.

3 And dost thou think this, O man, that judgest those who do such things and *doest the same*, that thou shalt escape the judgment of God?

> If a child of ours accuses his sister of wrongdoing, all the while knowing he committed the very same wrongdoing, aren't both in the wrong and shouldn't the son suffer the same consequence as his sister and perhaps even more so because he blamed his sister without acknowledging his own sin?
>
> Judging others while actively committing the same sin should be an obvious error to avoid, yet it was necessary to put this into writing to make all things clear to those who wish to serve the Lord in honesty, and to keep order in the Church. We tend to be too much like children and sometimes it's embarrassing what all had to be put into the Bible – things that are obvious, yet if not spelled out clearly, we might take advantage for the lack of clarity. But now we are not excusable for any sin, and especially so if we know enough to point out right and wrong in others.

4 Or dost thou despise the riches of his goodness and forbearance and longsuffering, ignoring that the goodness of God leads thee to repentance?

5 But after thy hardness and impenitent heart treasures up unto thyself wrath against the day of wrath and revelation of the righteous judgment of God,

"The goodness of God leads us to repentance" (v. 4). This does not say that the goodness of God looks the other way when we sin. No, rather it says that God leads us to *repentance*. To *repent* means to stop what we are doing, to turn from the wrong direction in which we were heading, to go God's way, being faithful to Him who leads us in the paths of righteousness.

6 who will render to everyone according to his deeds:

7 to those who persevered in well doing, glory and honour and incorruption, to those who seek eternal life;

8 but unto those that are contentious and do not obey the truth, but are persuaded by unrighteousness, indignation and wrath.

Romans is known to be the book of grace. Yet if we take an objective look at the words here, it is clear that *those who persevered in well doing* are the ones who receive *glory and honor and incorruption* (v. 7).

Likewise, verse 8 makes is clear that it is the disobedient who will not be rewarded with eternal life.

9 Tribulation and anguish *shall be* upon every human soul that does evil, the Jew first and also the Greek;

10 but glory, honour, and peace to everyone that works good, to the Jew first and also to the Greek.

11 For there is no respect of persons with God.

12 For as many as have sinned without law shall also

perish without law, and as many as have sinned in the law shall be judged by the law

> God is not a respecter of persons (v. 11), and no matter our background or the teaching we have received, we will be held accountable for the life we have lived. There are no exceptions. If we lived for the Lord in word and in deed, a reward awaits us. If we lived for ourselves or for the praise of men, if we willfully lived in sin and took advantage of others for our own gain, *tribulation and anguish* await us (v. 9).

> Nowhere in any of his writings does Paul teach that we can live in sin and escape the consequences. Grace was extended to us in the form of Jesus Christ, yet if we sin openly or hidden in our hearts, we are guilty. If we truly love God with all our heart, soul, mind, and strength, we will certainly also *work good* (v. 10).

13 (for not the hearers of the law *are* just before God, but the doers of the law shall be justified;

14 for when the Gentiles, who do not have the law, do by nature that which is of the law, these, not having the law, are a law unto themselves;

15 which show the work of the law written in their hearts, their conscience also bearing witness, accusing and also excusing their reasonings one with another)

16 in the day when God shall judge that which men have covered up, according to my gospel by Jesus, the Christ.

Many know *about* God, but yet don't *know* God, and certainly aren't known *of* God. There is a day coming when mere professors of faith will be exposed and only the true children of God will *be justified*.

Such straightforward speaking as Paul is doing in this chapter is seldom found with many pastors and teachers of today, perhaps because it sounds offensive. But by speaking all truth, Paul helps rather than hinders, and the truth is only offensive to evil-doers. It is imperative that the church understands and teaches the truth regarding how important being a "doer of the law" is, yet also being careful to teach that we must build solely on the foundation of Jesus Christ. Some will reason away these early chapters in Romans, saying that later chapters eliminate the importance of holy, sanctified living. Not so. Rather, these chapters help the book of Romans be conclusive, working together in a complete and comprehensive letter to the Romans.

17 ¶ Behold, thou doth call thyself a Jew and art supported by the law and doth glory in God

18 and dost know *his* will and approve the things that are more excellent, being instructed out of the law,

19 and art confident that thou thyself art *a* guide of the blind, *a* light of those who *are* in darkness,

20 an instructor of the ignorant, a teacher of children, who hast the form of knowledge and of the truth in the law.

21 Thou, therefore, who teachest another, teachest thou not thyself? Thou that preachest a man should not steal, dost thou steal?

22 Thou that sayest a man should not commit adultery, dost thou commit adultery? Thou that dost abhor idols, dost thou commit sacrilege?

23 Thou that makest thy boast of the law, with rebellion to the law doth thou dishonour God?

> Paul is addressing a very real problem. These people knew the scriptures, and preached to others that they must obey God. In fact, they held others to a very high, biblical standard and condemned them if they fell short. Yet, it is important to notice that Paul does not condemn the high standards. Rather, he's condemning the lack of following the same standards being taught to others, resulting in the name of God being blasphemed by the teachers (v. 24).
>
> We can be sure that our sin will be found out, both by other men and by God (Numbers 32:23), and will be held even more accountable if we have double standards, one for others, and a lesser standard for ourselves.

24 For the name of God is blasphemed among the Gentiles through you, as it is written.

25 For circumcision verily profits if thou keep the law, but if thou art a rebel to the law, thy circumcision is made *into* a foreskin.

26 Therefore if the uncircumcised keep the righteousness of the law, shall not his foreskin be counted for circumcision?

27 And that which is by nature foreskin, but keeps the law perfectly, shall judge thee who with the letter and with the circumcision art rebellious to the law.

28 For he is not a Jew who is one outwardly, neither is circumcision that which is done outwardly in the flesh;

29 but he *is* a Jew who is one inwardly, and circumcision *is that* of the heart, in the spirit *and* not in the letter, whose praise is not of men, but of God.

> What is God looking at? V. 27 makes it clear that we must have a clean heart, a heart free from our natural flesh, being *circumcised of the heart.* Only then will we have praise of God (v. 29). If we follow the law perfect outwardly, yet not inwardly, and if we care for the praise of men rather than God, we will fall short of what is necessary to gain eternal life.

Romans 3

1 ¶ What advantage then has the Jew? or what profit *is there* of circumcision?

2 Much in every way: first, certainly, that the oracles of God have been entrusted unto them.

> In Romans 3, Paul makes it clear that we are justified by faith in the blood of Jesus Christ, for the remission of sins (v. 25). However, lest people misunderstand and reject the Jews to whom the law was given, Paul makes it very clear that God's heart is for the Jews and that the law is a desirable and good thing (confirmed in v. 31).

3 For what if some of them did not believe? Shall their unbelief have made the truth of God without effect?

4 No, in no wise: for God is true, and every man a liar; as it is written, That thou might be justified in thy words and might overcome when thou dost judge.

5 And if our iniquity commends the righteousness

of God, what shall we say? Shall *for this reason* God be unjust who sends punishment? (I speak as a man.)

6 No, in no wise: for then how shall God judge the world?

7 For if the truth of God has more abounded through my lie unto his glory, why even so am I also judged as a sinner?

8 And why not say (as we are slanderously reported, and as some affirm that we say), Let us do evil, that good may come? The condemnation of whom is just.

> *...our iniquity commends the righteousness of God* (v. 5). Does this mean we ought to sin, so that it is more obvious that God is holy? Not so, as v. 8 confirms. Yet, by the very fact that we are sinners, and some hardened against God, we do magnify the holiness of God and all this fits into God's purposes for creating man. That the wickedness of man illuminates the holiness of God is a truth that will become very clear in Romans 9. What Paul is revealing here is a behind-the-scenes picture of what was necessary to again create order in the heavens, something that was disrupted when Lucifer and one-third of the angels rebelled against God. Creation and all that has happened since is much more about God than it is about us, and everything that has happened and is happening is for God's purposes and for His glory. Yet we are also held accountable for our sins, as is also necessary and right. How this all is true and fits together may be a mystery to us, but just because we don't understand it doesn't give us

a right to disregard what Paul by divine inspiration is saying to us here.

9 What then? Are we better *than they*? No, in no wise; for we have before proved both Jews and Gentiles that they are all under sin;

10 as it is written, There is no one righteous, no, not one;

11 there is no one that understands; there is no one that seeks after God.

12 They are all gone out of the way; they are together become unprofitable; there is no one that does good, no, not one.

13 Their throat *is* an open sepulchre; with their tongues they have used deceit; the poison of asps *is* under their lips,

14 whose mouth *is* full of cursing and bitterness;

15 their feet *are* swift to shed blood;

16 destruction and misery *are* in their ways,

17 and the way of peace they have not known;

18 there is no fear of God before their eyes.

The seriousness and vastness of humanity's rebellion against God is clearly presented here. This is far different from what society, and even Christians, would have us believe – that we are basically good and well-intentioned people and that we need to believe in ourselves and other people more in order to accomplish something good in this world.

It is necessary to see things as they really are from God's perspective, it doesn't help to flatter anyone with things that aren't true. The reality is that we are *all under sin*. Some will error inversely and think and talk only about how bad people are and end up being so negative that they don't love their brothers and sisters in Christ because of their flaws.

As we are reading this, we must have an objective view of truth and not forget any components of the whole. Paul is making a well-rounded presentation, not leaving any room for error. He writes concisely, which means we must not read too fast or skip any single verse, as skipping key verses or words can cause us to become off-balanced and unbiblical in our understanding of the scriptures.

19 ¶ Now we know that all that the law says, it says to those who are under the law, that every mouth may be stopped, and all the world may submit themselves unto God.

20 For by the deeds of the law, no flesh shall be justified in his sight; for by the law *is* the knowledge of sin.

21 But now, without the law, the righteousness of God has been manifested, being witnessed by the law and the prophets:

22 the righteousness, that is, of God by the faith of

Jesus, the Christ, for all and upon all those that believe in him, for there is no difference;

> Our *mouths will be stopped* (v. 19) when we encounter the truth about our sinfulness before God. Naturally, people like nothing better than to talk about themselves, and can talk endlessly about their personal plans, their work, and even their good deeds. But a true encounter with the law of God stops the mouths of even the most selfish individual.

> Praise God, *the righteousness of God has been manifested, being witness by the law and the prophets* (v. 21). Both the law and the prophets have pointed to a coming Messiah, the worthy one who would live without sin, and in obedience to the Father would die as the ultimate sacrifice for sin. It is faith in His sacrifice (v. 25), and it is His righteousness that we put on (Matthew 22:11-14), and it is Him whom we follow while on earth (1 Peter 2:21). *Be ye holy; for I am holy* (1 Peter 1:16).

23 for all have sinned and are made destitute of the glory of God,

24 *being* justified freely by his grace through the redemption that is in Jesus, the Christ,

25 whom God purposed for reconciliation through faith in his blood for the manifestation of his righteousness, for the remission of sins that are past, by the patience of God,

> God's grace came in the form of Jesus Christ (v. 24),

and outside of Christ, there is no grace or mercy for humanity. Some say we should be patient with sinners, first building a relationship and only interject bits and pieces of the Gospel as opportunity arises. While there is an element of truth to this, what is often meant is that we ought not to offend people with the truth. The truth is that we all as sinners are an offence to God, if we are found outside of Christ. Hence, it is imperative that we lead sinners to our Lord and Savior, Jesus Christ, the only place where sinners can find mercy and grace, and there must be conviction of sin and true repentance before this can take place.

...for the remission of sins that are <u>past</u> (v. 25). Jesus Christ died once for all, but He did not die so that we may continue in sin. This is why scripture says *For if we sin wilfully after we have received the knowledge of the truth, there remains no more sacrifice for sins* (Hebrews 10:26). The teaching that Jesus Christ died for all sins past, present, and future, is simply not true. Whereas it is true that there is no forgiveness for sins outside of Jesus Christ's one-time sacrifice, this does not mean that we can continue in sin and expect our new sins to automatically be covered by the blood (v. 8).

26 manifesting in this time his righteousness that he *only* be the just *one* and the justifier of him that is of the faith of Jesus.

27 Where is boasting then? It is excluded. By what law? of works? No, but by *the* law of faith.

28 Therefore, we conclude that *a* man is justified by faith without the deeds of the law.

> As we can see clearly, we are *justified by faith without the deeds of the law* (v. 28). But how does this reconcile with Romans 2, where Paul says *the doers of the law shall be justified* (Romans 2:13)? Here we begin what seems to be a contradiction of truths. On one hand, we are held accountable to our deeds. On the other hand, we are not justified by works, but by faith. But this isn't as impossible as it sounds. Let the words say what they say where they say it, and let the truth be according to the words you read. These are not opposing contradictions, but a full and complete truth. One truth doesn't cancel the other out, and neither does one truth meet the other in the middle, and yet both sides are true in their own right.

29 *Is he* the God of the Jews only? *Is he* not also of the Gentiles? Yes, of the Gentiles also,

30 seeing *it is* one God who shall justify the circumcision by faith and *the* uncircumcision by faith.

31 Do we then make void the law through faith? No, in no wise; to the contrary, we establish the law.

> Paul makes it clear that even though we are justified by faith, we do not *make void the law through faith*. This is a deep, yet refreshing and exciting reality,

and we'll continue to see all pieces of this intricate puzzle fit together as we continue in this study. The aim to see all of God's word as true, reconcilable, and profitable for the body of Christ.

Romans 4

1 ¶ What shall we say then that Abraham our father, as pertaining to the flesh, has found?

2 For if Abraham were justified by works, he has *reason* to glory *in himself*, but not before God.

> It is imperative that God gets the glory, not mankind. Why? This is simply because we are God's creation and the creator gets the honor for his creation, rather than the creation itself (Hebrews 3:1-4). Furthermore, we have all sinned and fallen short of the glory of God and are not worthy even to be called sons of God. Our redemption is undeserved and unearned, and in no way can we claim credit for it. As unrealistic as it would be to think that we somehow cause the sun to rise each day, so unrealistic would it be to think we somehow earned our salvation.

3 For what does the scripture say? Abraham believed God, and it was counted unto him for righteousness.

> The threshold for salvation is relatively low (belief), and yet at the same time it is very difficult. So humbling and self-denying is this requirement that few enter in. But the one who climbs in some other way is a thief and robber and will be cast out, having no part in the kingdom of God (John 10:1; Matthew 7:23).

4 But unto him that works, the reward is not reckoned as grace, but as debt.

> When we sin, it is often impossible to actually pay back the debt we owe to others for our sins. For example, if I kill a husband and father (through an accident due to negligence on my part, for the sake of this example), it is impossible by my work to restore the man to his wife and children. I might be very sorry or even support them financially, but that is not enough – the husband and father himself cannot possibly be restored to life and to his family. So it is with us and God – we have sinned so greatly, and so great is our debt, that we cannot repay the actual debt that we owe.

5 But to him that does not work, but believes in him that justifies the ungodly, the faith is counted as righteousness.

> God offered us forgiveness through His Son who took the death penalty that we ourselves deserved by shedding His own blood, taking our place on the cross on which we deserved to die. By faith in Christ, accepting God's forgiveness offered through Christ,

we may be forgiven for our sin. *Greater love has no man than this, that a man lay down his soul for his friends* (John 15:13), and that is what Jesus did for us by obedience to the Father through the cross.

6 Even as David also describes the blessedness of the man unto whom God doth attribute righteousness without works,

7 *saying*, Blessed *are* those whose iniquities are forgiven and whose sins are covered.

8 Blessed *is* the man to whom the Lord does not impute sin.

> How often we hear people talking of blessings that come in the form of friends and family, work and possessions, health and safety. But when we come to grips with the reality of our sin, how very much we will realize that we are most blessed to not be punished for our sins.
>
> If we were on death row, awaiting the due consequence for our sin, we would perhaps understand what it means to receive a pardon instead of execution. The earthly possessions we once called blessings will pale in value when compared to the pardon we received. When we think of our past, it will be the pardon that we'll praise God for and tell others about. That particular day when we received the pardon will stand out as grander than the day we were born, and we will be thankful to no other person more than the one whom granted the pardon.

9 ¶ Is this blessedness, therefore, only upon the circumcision or also upon the uncircumcision? for we say that faith was reckoned to Abraham as righteousness.

10 How was it then reckoned? when he was in circumcision or in uncircumcision? Not in circumcision, but in uncircumcision.

11 And he received the circumcision as *a* sign, as *a* seal of the righteousness of the faith which *he had, yet* being uncircumcised, that he might be the father of all the uncircumcised believers, that it might be counted unto them also as righteousness,

> Abraham *received the circumcision as a sign* and *a seal* of the righteousness he received by faith. Are there outward signs when we believe? Absolutely. In fact, if there is no outward change in the one who says they believe in Jesus Christ, we would have reason to question whether or not they believed at all. Yet it is never the outward sign itself that saves us, but *faith* (v. 9).

12 that *he be* the father of the circumcision: not only to those who are of the circumcision, but also unto those who walk in the steps of the faith that was in our father Abraham before he was circumcised.

13 For the promise that he should be the heir of the world *was* not to Abraham or to his seed through the law, but through the righteousness of faith.

> Who can be saved? *Those who walk in the steps of faith* (v. 12) that Abraham walked in, and it's to be

noted that Abraham was found faithful (and justified) *before* he was circumcised. Note the phrase *steps of faith*, indicating a real walking out of our inward faith.

14 For if those who are of the law *are* the heirs, faith is *in* vain, and the promise annulled,

If salvation were based on a family name, an inheritance passed down from generation to generation, anyone outside the family could have no hope. However, the promise wasn't only those who are of the law (the sons of Israel), but to everyone *through the righteousness of faith*.

15 because the law works wrath; for where there is no law, *there is* no rebellion either.

The fastest way to test rebellion is to enact a law. Before there was a law, perhaps only a few people were tempted to do the thing the law was to prevent. But put a law in place, and those who are bold will break the law purposely, and those who are not as brave will talk and joke about doing so, and even weak Christians will do so.

16 Therefore by faith, that *it might be* by grace, to the end the promise might be sure to all *the* seed, not only to that which is of the law, but also to that which is of the faith of Abraham, who is the father of us all,

17 ¶ as it is written, As a father of many Gentiles have I placed thee before God, whom he believed, who gives life to the dead and calls those things which are not as those that are.

18 Who believed to wait against *all* hope, that he might become the father of many Gentiles, according to that which had been spoken *unto him*, So shall thy seed be.

19 And he did not weaken in faith: he considered not his own body now dead when he was about one hundred years old, neither yet the deadness of Sara's womb;

> Here is faith, that we see beyond the deadness of our own body (and we truly are dead in our sins), and believe God that life can spring forth from our deadness (we can be alive with Christ in His resurrection). Rarely can we see past the physical, yet that is just what Abraham did.

> The promise to Abraham was first that he would *be a father of many Gentiles* (Genesis 17:4), so that it would first be righteousness by faith. But the covenant was established with Abraham's son Isaac second (Genesis 17:21), and the fulfillment of the law (Jesus Christ) came through that family.

20 he doubted not the promise of God, with unbelief, but was strengthened in faith, giving glory to God,

21 being fully persuaded that he was also powerful to do all that he had promised;

> Do we believe that God is able to do all that He promised? You perhaps believe that the Lord saved you from your sin, but do you believe that He can

give you strength to overcome sin and the world? Do you believe that He is able to keep you until the day of your death and through your dying hours? Do you lean on Him for provision in this life now, and to provide all things for your spouse and children if you die? If we cannot add a single hair to our head, then it stands to reason that we must lean on all the promises of God for life and godliness.

22 therefore, *his faith* was also attributed unto him as righteousness.

> We are not righteous because we believe, but righteousness is *attributed* to us because we believe. The difference seems minor, but it is significant. Most, believers and unbelievers alike, think they are basically good people, but we must remember that even if we have faith, righteousness is merely attributed to us. Righteousness is not our own, but it is *attributed* to us if we have Christ.

23 ¶ Now it is not written for his sake alone that it was *so* reckoned to him,

24 but for us also to whom it shall be *so* reckoned, that is, to those that believe in him that raised up Jesus our Lord from the dead,

25 who was delivered for our offenses and was raised again for our justification.

> When reconciling my bank account, the credits must balance perfectly with the debits. By His death, Christ was delivered for our offenses. By His

resurrection, we are justified (v. 25), or reconciled. It is through His death that the ultimate price was paid. It is through His life that we now live and have hope for the future. All praise and honor and glory is Christ's, for He is the balancer of our account with God.

Romans 5

1 ¶ Justified therefore by faith, we have peace with God through our Lord Jesus, the Christ,

2 by whom we also have access by faith into this grace in which we stand and glory in hope of the glory *of the sons* of God.

> We have *peace* and *grace* with God in no other way than through our *Lord Jesus, the Christ*.

3 And not only *this*, but we even glory in the tribulations, knowing that the tribulation works patience;

4 and patience, experience; and experience, hope;

5 and the hope shall not be ashamed, because the love of God is poured out in our hearts by the Holy Spirit which is given unto us.

> How rare it is to hear a Christian *glory in tribulation*. Even pastors, missionaries, and other Christian workers are seldom content in tribulation. But if we

let it, tribulation generates patience, which results in experience, which makes hope come alive. We will not be ashamed with the end result, even if the current tribulation seems shameful.

If you are suffering because you stand for what is true and because you exalt the name of Jesus Christ, give thanks for the fact that you are counted worthy to suffer for His name's sake (Acts 5:41). Only make sure that you are suffering for Christ's sake, and not because of wrongdoing.

6 ¶ For the Christ, when we were yet weak, in his time died for the ungodly.

7 For scarcely for a righteous man will one die, yet peradventure for a good man some would even dare to die.

8 But God increased the price of his charity toward us in that while we were yet sinners the Christ died for us.

Who would you die for? Your family? Your country? Perhaps, but would you die for your enemy? Suppose someone is against you in every way and mocked you even though you did nothing wrong. Would you die for that person if the need arose? That is what God did for us by sending His son to die for us while we were still in our rebellion against Him. That is how very much God *increased His charity towards us*, going above and beyond what seems reasonable.

Yet despite this, mankind still holds out that God is unfair, unjust, and unloving. Despite the greatest charity (undeserved love) known to man, hardhearted men still refuse it, choosing instead to go their own way, to their own bitter end.

9 Then much more now justified in his blood, we shall be saved from wrath by him.

10 For if, when we were enemies, we were reconciled with God by the death of his Son, much more, *now* reconciled, we shall be saved by his life.

> We are reconciled to God by the death of His Son. One debit (Adam's sin) plus one credit (Christ's death) equals reconciliation. But it doesn't stop with a balancing of the scales with our gracious Father. He not only reconciles us through His Son's death, He gives us than we deserve – eternal life through the resurrection and life of Jesus Christ!

11 And not only this, but we even glory in God through our Lord Jesus, the Christ, by whom we have now received the reconciliation.

12 Therefore, in the manner which sin entered into the world by one man, and because of sin, death; and so death passed upon all men in the one in whom all sinned.

> The debit that occurred when Adam sinned was passed on to all humanity. This is apparent even in our own children – as soon as they can talk, their sinful nature soon shows up in many ways. Sin results in death. Even a practical look at sin reveals this – most sin results in poor health and shorten

THE EPISTLE OF THE APOSTLE PAUL TO THE ROMANS

life expectancy, and almost without fail, the sins of fathers are passed on to their children.

13 For until the law, sin was in the world; but the sin was not imputed, *there* being no law.

14 Nevertheless death reigned from Adam to Moses, even in those that did not sin after the manner of the rebellion of Adam, who is a figure of him that was to come.

> David said this: *They are all gone aside, they are all together become filthy: there is no one that does good, no, not one* (Psalm 14:3). God's law shows us that we are sinners (Romans 7:7), but here (v. 14), it is even evident that Adam's sin was passed on to all mankind in that from Adam to Moses, even when there was no law that magnified sin and despite the fact that not all people from Adam until Moses sinned in the same way Adam did (there were some good people who lived between Adam and Moses), and this was also before the law was even given by Moses, yet they were all still found guilty before God.

15 But not as the offense, so also *is* the gift. For if through the offense of *that* one many died, much more the grace of God and the gift by the grace of one man, Jesus the Christ, has abounded unto many.

16 Nor was it in the same manner as by one sin, likewise also the gift; for the judgment truly *came* of one *sin* unto condemnation, but grace *came* of many offenses unto justification.

17 For if by one offense, death reigned *because* of one *man*; much more those who receive the abundance of grace and of gifts and of righteousness shall reign in life by one, Jesus the Christ.

18 Therefore, in the same manner that by the iniquity of one *guilt came* upon all men unto condemnation, even so by the righteousness of one, *grace came* upon all men unto justification of life.

> Paul makes it abundantly clear that we are reconciled through Christ, almost in repetition ,yet with enough variation in his explanations so that every possible angle is covered and making it clear who man is reconciled. This issue of how man may be reconciled with God and receive the life of Christ is not to be taken lightly or skimmed over when reading. It is only through Christ that we may be one with God again.

19 For as by one man's disobedience, many were made sinners, so by the obedience of one shall many be made righteous.

20 Moreover the law entered that the offence might abound. But where sin abounded, grace did much more abound,

21 so that in the same manner as sin has reigned unto death, even so might grace reign through righteousness unto eternal life by Jesus, the Christ, our Lord.

> *Eternal life by Jesus, the Christ, our Lord.* What a gift was given to us! We do well if we are able to make

it our highest goal to believe in and honor our Lord and Savior Jesus Christ with all our being. He alone gets the credit for our salvation and our eternal life. He alone deserves our praise and our thanks and He alone is worthy.

Romans 6

1 ⁋ What shall we say then? Shall we continue in sin that grace may abound?

2 No, in no wise. How shall we that are dead to sin live any longer therein?

> It sometimes helps to ask ourselves "What if this had not been added to the Bible?" It was necessary to add this passage of scripture to make it clear that we are not free to continue in sin ,no matter how much grace we were given. It's even a little embarrassing that God through Paul had to make sure this is spelled out clearly, yet it was necessary, or otherwise some would've taken advantage of grace. We were given grace in that Christ died for us, to pay the penalty for our sins, but we were not given grace so that we might continue sinning without consequence.
>
> Unfortunately, despite what is said here, some Christians still think they are free to continue in

sin. This is happening because of incomplete or even heretical teachings, or simply because a Christian has a sin problem and doesn't know how or isn't willing to deal with it. What seems to be the easy way out is to say that Jesus died on the cross for "all my sin – past, present, and future," but in reality, this is not what the Bible says.

To say that we may continue in sin would be like saying a murderer, when pardoned by a governor, should be allowed to continue murdering people because of the pardon he received. That is a ridiculous thought, and it is just as ridiculous to think that we are given liberty to continue in sin after we have believed in Christ.

3 Know ye not that all of us that are baptized into Jesus the Christ are baptized into his death?

4 For we are buried with him by baptism into death, that just as the Christ was raised up from the dead to the glory of the Father, likewise we also walk in newness of life.

5 For if we have been planted together *in him* in the likeness of his death, we shall be also *in the likeness* of *his* resurrection,

> If we are genuinely identified with Christ, we are identified with Him in death and must recon ourselves dead to our old ways and alive through Christ's resurrection.
>
> Read the gospels and take note of the words Jesus

spoke and how He related to others after the resurrection. There is a marked difference – even in His perfection before death and resurrection He set an example of the difference we should expect after our conversion. We must *be in the likeness of his resurrection.* Not the same as Jesus Christ, as He is the one and only Savior of the world, but in the *likeness of His resurrection.* This implies not acting like Him, or being little christs as perhaps some think, but yet it is expected to see similarities in ourselves as a result of the life He imparts to us.

6 knowing this: that our old man is crucified with *him* that the body of sin might be destroyed that we should not serve sin any longer.

7 For he that is dead is justified from sin.

> What was it that we were delivered from by Christ's death? Sin! We are in no way led to believe that sin is to be an expected part of a Christian's life. The thing we were delivered from, the *body of sin*, is to remain dead and not resurrect with our new life. Satan and our flesh will both work to destroy what was done at the cross, but we must resist the devil so that he flees from us (James 4:7). Praise God, through Christ we are given the power to resist the temptations to sin.

8 Now if we die with the Christ, we believe that we shall also live with him,

9 knowing that the Christ, having been raised from

the dead, dies no more; death has no more dominion over him.

10 For *he* that is dead died unto sin once, and *he* that lives, lives unto God.

> There will be no second atonement (v. 9-10). What happened on the cross happened once. If *we die with the Christ* and *we believe that we shall also live with him*, then we must make this truth a foremost principle in our living. It is not so much wresting to believe this is true as it is acknowledging and accepting that it is true, and bringing our body (flesh) and our mind (thoughts) into subjection to the truth.

11 Likewise also reckon yourselves to be truly dead unto sin, but alive unto God in Christ, Jesus, our Lord.

12 Therefore do not let sin reign in your mortal body that ye should obey it in the lusts thereof.

> We must *reckon* ourselves to be dead unto sin, we must account for this be true since God says it is true.

> We must say "no" to sin when the temptation rises up, instead living unto God through Christ. …*do not let sin reign* implies that we must use our mind and or bodily strength in order to not *obey the lusts* of our *mortal body*. Does this take effort? Yes. It takes more effort than some are willing to exert, but the statement *do not let sin reign* in verse 12 makes it clear that must we undertake this battle, and that we also have access to the spiritual resources needed to win the battle.

13 Neither present your members *as* instruments of unrighteousness unto sin, but present yourselves unto God as those that are alive from the dead and your members *as* instruments of righteousness unto God.

> We gladly blame the devil and our old nature for our sin, but rare is the Christian who accepts the blame for his own sins. But Paul is so bold as to say that we should not *present* our *members as instruments of unrighteousness*, as if we are stepping forward and volunteering that the devil use our bodies to play an unrighteous tune of sin.

14 So that sin shall have no dominion over you; for ye are not under the law, but under grace.

15 What then? shall we sin because we are not under the law, but under grace? No, in no wise.

> Paul again feels the need to make it clear that sin must not have dominion over us. Does this "shall not" mean that sin can't have dominion over us because God's grace towards us somehow perpetually cleanses us from sin? I don't think so. What Paul is saying here is that we are to take a stand against sin. *No, in no wise.* In no possible way shall we allow ourselves to sin.

16 Or know ye not that to whom ye present yourselves slaves to obey, his slaves ye are to whom ye obey, whether of sin unto death or of the obedience unto righteousness?

17 Thank God that, although ye were the slaves of sin,

ye have obeyed from the heart that form of doctrine unto which ye are delivered;

18 and freed from sin, ye are become the slaves of righteousness.

> While we were slaves to sin in the past, we are now *slaves of righteousness* (v. 18). If one is a slave, he is bound to his master; and if righteousness is our master, then we are bound to and must be righteous. No more can we be set free, nor should we want to, than a slave could be set free from his master in biblical times.
>
> The doctrine of slavery is not popular in today's culture, but slavery was necessary so we could get a picture of what it means to be bought with a price, and not be our own. We are not free in the sense of being able to do whatever we want, but we are the Lord's. While this concept is resisted by many, those who love their Master will find that no greater slave-owner ever existed. In fact, a day with Lord is as a thousand elsewhere (Psalm 84:10), meaning that in whatever capacity we find ourselves, not a single day in the best earthly capacity is worth a thousand-to-one compared to being with our master, the Lord and Savior Jesus Christ.

19 I speak a human thing because of the weakness of our flesh: that as ye presented your members to serve uncleanness and iniquity unto iniquity, likewise now present your members to serve righteousness unto holiness.

20 For being *previously* the slaves of sin, *now* ye have been made the slaves of righteousness.

> While we *presented our members to serve uncleanness unto iniquity,* we now must *present our members to serve righteousness unto holiness.* We're not as weak as we think we are, and we don't "fall" into sin. Instead, the reality is that we present ourselves to sin; but if we are in Christ, we must now *present* ourselves as instruments of righteousness. Remaining neutral isn't an option listed here. Instead, we must gather up ourselves and say "Here am I, Lord" (1 Samuel 3) and allow Him to play a beautiful tune of holiness with our lives.

21 What fruit had ye then in those things of which ye are now ashamed? for the end of those things *is* death.

> If we are not ashamed of our past sins, then we have not fully understood the wickedness of unholy living. The way of the ungodly and the sinner is death (1 Peter 4:18). But praise God, our past wickedness doesn't have to be the end of the story.

22 But now freed from sin and made slaves to God, ye have as your fruit sanctification and as the end, everlasting life.

23 For the wages of sin *is* death, but the grace of God *is* eternal life in Christ Jesus our Lord.

> The truth is clear: *the wages of sin is death* (v. 23). There is no good news and no rejoicing for the sinner. But, there is good news: Grace came in the

form of Jesus Christ, and the invitation is to all to come forward and receive His precious gift of death on the cross for our sins and eternal life by His resurrection. Beneficiaries of Christ's death and resurrection, and *slaves to God* (v. 22), we have *sanctification* and *everlasting life*). Amen!

Romans 7

1 ¶ Know ye not, brethren (for I speak to those that know the law), that the law has dominion over a man *only* as long as he lives?

2 For the woman who is subject to a husband is obligated to the law so long as the husband lives; but if the husband dies, she is free from the law of the husband.

> Do you know the law (v. 1)? If not, read through the Bible and carefully watch the words as you read. Don't easily dismiss any of it, as is too often done by both the churched and the unchurched. The churched are taught to over-contextualize everything (basically explaining away much of scripture) and the unchurched often simply don't believe what they read. But it is important to be aware that the text itself, in its original form, was intended to be read verbatim. Read and believe the words you read and you will *know the law.*

> In the Bible, the husband is a type of Christ and the

wife is a type of the Church. The Church is sadly ignorant of this truth, and as a result, Christian couples are getting divorced as remarried about as much as the world. Christ would never divorce His bride and He expects us to maintain that type in our own marriages.

The woman (the Church) is only free to get remarried after her husband dies. We are only freed from our union with the flesh and the law when the old man dies. But then, praise the Lord, we are free to be join to another, this time to Christ.

3 So then if, while *her* husband lives, she belongs to another man, she shall be called an adulteress; but if her husband dies, she is free from that law so that she is no adulteress if she belongs to another man.

4 Likewise ye also, my brethren, are become dead to the law in the body of the Christ that ye should belong to another, *even* to him who is raised from the dead, that we should bring forth fruit unto God.

When we die to the law, praise the Lord, we are free from the old man, who is dead in sins! No longer do we serve the law of sin and death, but we are to bear *fruit unto God* (v. 4). Yet sadly, many who claim the name of Christ are still serving the flesh, essentially looking back to the old instead of looking only to *him who is raised from the dead* (v. 4).

5 For while we were in the flesh, the affections of the

sins which were by the law worked in our members to bring forth fruit unto death.

> The fruit of the flesh is by nature sin. That's not to say that we can't do anything "good" in the flesh, but yet the nature of flesh is to produce sin. Simply look at your life before Christ, and it will be obvious that the general fruit of that life was sinful and far short of the holiness of God.

6 But now we are free from the law of death in which we were held, that we might serve in newness of Spirit, and not *in* the oldness of the letter.

7 ¶ What shall we say then? *Is* the law sin? No, in no wise. But, I did not know sin except by the law; for *neither* would I have known lust if the law did not say, Thou shalt not covet.

8 Then sin, when there was occasion by the commandment, wrought in me all manner of lust. For without the law sin was as if it were dormant.

> Is the law itself sin? Not at all. There isn't a single one of the ten commandments that isn't good. Yet, if it were possible for us to follow the law perfectly, it would only be for the good of ourselves and others. What we are set free from, then, is who we serve. We no longer serve the law of sin and death. Paul makes it very clear that the law itself isn't what is bad (v. 7), but that the law is a measuring stick to show us that we are sinners. Before Christ, we are

married to the law, and it is necessary for it to be so, in order for us to know that we are sinners (v. 8).

Before Christ, I was convicted of sin and my conscience pricked me when I sinned. I couldn't get away from it. I read the Bible and it mostly showed me how far I was from perfection. Now though, I serve Christ and do so out of love. As Christians, if we love the Lord Jesus Christ, we will serve Him diligently and unceasingly because we love Him, not just because of what the law says we should or should not do.

9 So that without the law I lived for some time; but when the commandment came, sin revived, and I died.

10 And I found that the *same* commandment, which was unto life, was mortal *unto me*.

11 For sin, having had occasion, deceived me by the commandment and by it killed *me*.

12 So the law is truly holy, and the commandment holy and just and good.

13 Was then that which is good made death unto me? No, in no wise. But sin, to show itself sin by that which is good, worked death in me, making sin exceedingly sinful by the commandment.

We live in a day when society wishes to do away with the commandments. Why? If the commandments are displayed, they convict individuals of sin. And with conviction of sin comes the realization that consequences are to follow, both in this life and in eternity.

Paul makes it abundantly clear that the law is good (v. 12) and in no way should we despise the law or teach others that the law is irrelevant. Jesus said, *Whosoever therefore shall undo one of these least commandments and shall teach men so, he shall be called the least in the kingdom of the heavens; but whosoever shall do and teach them, the same shall be called great in the kingdom of the heavens* (Matthew 5:19).

14 ¶ For we *now* know that the law is spiritual, but I am carnal, sold unto subjection by sin.

15 For that which I do, I do not understand, and not even the *good* that I desire *is what* I do; but what I hate, that *is what* I do.

16 If then I do that which I do not desire, I approve that the law *is* good.

17 So that it is no longer I that do it, but sin that dwells in me.

18 And I know that in me (that is, in my flesh) dwells no good thing; for I have the desire, but I am not able to perform that which is good.

19 For I do not do the good that I desire; but the evil which I do not desire, that I do.

20 And if I do that which I do not desire, I am not working, but sin that dwells in me.

21 So that, desiring to do good, I find *this* law: evil is natural unto me.

> *Evil is natural to me* (v. 21). How stark, but true! Evil is what we tend towards. Our flesh can never be trusted. Leave us to ourselves, and we will wander into all sorts of evil. But praise God, He has also made a way of escape (1 Corinthians 10:13).

22 For I delight with the law of God with the inward man,

23 but I see another law in my members which rebels against the law of my mind, bringing captive unto the law of sin which is in my members.

> If I let the *law in my members* (my flesh) go without restraint, I will sin. When we are born again and receive the Holy Spirit, our flesh still fights to live, but yet it can and must be in subjection to our spirit. Paul said *I keep my body under, and bring it into subjection, lest preaching to others, I myself should become reprobate* (1 Corinthians 9:27). Jesus said, *If anyone will come after me, let him deny himself and take up his cross and follow me* (Matthew 16:24).

> The scriptures consistently make the case that we must deny the lusts of the flesh and follow Christ. There is no good thing that dwells in us (Romans 7:18), and Paul is making it abundantly clear that the desires of our flesh are only towards sin.

24 O wretched man that I am! who shall deliver me from the body of this death?

25 The grace of God, by Jesus, the Christ, our Lord. So then with the mind I myself serve the law of God, but with the flesh the law of sin.

> Praise the Lord, not only are we given a clear picture that our flesh is sinful, but we are also given the answer for deliverance from our *body of death.* The Lord Jesus Christ's death and resurrection is God's grace towards us, and if we deny ourselves and follow Him, the body of death, our flesh, will no longer get its own way.

Romans 8

1 ¶ So that now, *there is* no condemnation to those who are in Christ, Jesus, who walk not according to the flesh, but according to the Spirit.

> There is no condemnation if we are *in Christ*. If we are *in Christ*, we must also walk according to the Spirit. And when we walk *according to the Spirit*, we do not walk according to the flesh. The fruit of the flesh is only evil (Romans 7:28), and the fruit of the Spirit is only godly as the rest of this chapter will clearly show us. The distinction between the two is clear.

2 For the law of the Spirit of life in Christ, Jesus, has made me free from the law of sin and death.

3 For that which was impossible to the law, in that it was weak through the flesh, God sending his own Son in the likeness of sinful flesh and for sin, condemned sin in the flesh

> The weakness of the law is the flesh. The weakness of the law isn't the law itself, as the law is only good. What doesn't work about the law though, is us – our own corrupt, law-breaking flesh. It is necessary to be set *free from the law of sin and death*.

> It's of interest to note that Paul says here that Christ came and *condemned sin in the flesh* (v. 3). The law already showed us how sinful we were, how far short of the glory of God we were, yet when Christ came and took on *the likeness of sinful flesh*, He not only took our place by dying on the cross in our place, He also simultaneously condemned living according to the flesh.

4 that the righteousness of the law might be fulfilled in us who walk not according to the flesh, but according to the Spirit.

5 For those that are according to the flesh know the things that are of the flesh; but those that are according to the Spirit, the things that are of the Spirit.

> When is the righteousness of the law fulfilled? When *we walk according to the Spirit* (v. 3) which is only possible because of Christ.

6 For the prudence of the flesh *is* death, but the prudence of the Spirit, life and peace,

7 because the prudence of the flesh *is* enmity against God; for it does not subject itself to the law of God, neither indeed can it.

In this book of Romans, Paul makes a rock-solid, courtroom-proof case regarding sin and its cure. He's approaching truth from various angles and making sure there are no loop-holes left for error. Earlier (in Romans 6 and 7), Paul talks about the *fruit* of the flesh versus the *fruit* that results from walking according to the Spirit, very similar to what is being said in these verses.

8 So then, those that are carnal cannot please God.

9 But ye are not in the flesh, but in the Spirit, because the Spirit of God dwells in you. Now if anyone does not have the Spirit of Christ, that person is not of him.

It is of utmost importance to understand that we cannot please God in the flesh. Most evangelical churches preach Jesus Christ for our salvation, but it is a shame that there is less teaching regarding the mortifying of the flesh (v. 13).

We can, however, please God in the Spirit. The line is clear – we are either of the flesh, or we are of the Spirit. One is pleasing to God, the other an abomination to God.

10 ¶ But if Christ is in you, the body is truly dead because of sin, but the Spirit *is* alive because of righteousness.

11 And if the Spirit of him that raised up Jesus from the dead dwells in you, he that raised up the Christ from the dead shall also quicken your mortal bodies by his Spirit that dwells in you.

What has rendered our body dead? Sin (v. 10). Sin, by the commandment, slew us (Romans 7:11). Sin is the lethal poison that destroyed all holiness in our body, and all that is left is death. But, praise the Lord, if Christ is in us, the same Spirit that raised Him from the dead also quickens us, bringing us to vital, spiritual life.

12 Therefore, brethren, we are debtors, not to the flesh, to live according to the flesh.

This verse is a little tricky. It could be taken, as many do take it, that "we are debtors … to live according to the flesh." This would mean that we will live according to the flesh as long as we live on earth. However, that is clearly not what is meant. Even if you only read the verse immediately following this one (v. 13), you would see that this is not the case. It might be a more easily understandable rendering if it read something like "we are debtors, not to the flesh, *for we are debtors if we* live according to the flesh."

13 For if ye live according to the flesh, ye shall die; but if through the Spirit ye mortify the deeds of the body, ye shall live.

14 For all that are led by the Spirit of God, the same are sons of God.

It can't be more clear than this – if we are *led by the Spirit of God*, then we are sons of God. The Spirit will not lead us into error. But if we *live according to the flesh,* we will die. Stark words, perhaps, but unless the words are communicated clearly, how else will we know the truth? Also, this reality shouldn't scare us, as all that is required is that we repent and turn to God, and He will not withhold the Spirit from those who ask in sincerity.

Verse 13 says we need to *mortify the deeds of the body.* This is a spiritual battle, after all, and in a battle one side or the other wins. To obtain victory, the *deeds of the body* (flesh), must die. Will you fight this battle with spiritual means, not being willing to compromise with the enemy (our own flesh in this case)?

15 For ye have not received the spirit of slavery to be in fear *again*, but ye have received the Spirit of adoption *of sons*, whereby we cry, Abba, Father.

Amen. We do not receive a spirit of fear when we receive the Spirit of God. The Spirit of God makes us children of God, and as children of the most high God, we obtain the Spirit of peace, and are given the right to acknowledge Him as our Father.

16 For the same Spirit bears witness unto our spirit that we are sons of God,

17 ¶ and if sons, also heirs certainly of God and jointheirs with Christ, if so be that we suffer with *him* that we may be also glorified together *with him.*

18 For I know with certainty that the sufferings of this present time *are* not worthy *to be compared* with the coming glory which shall be manifested in us.

Not many Christians realize that being sons of God means that we will partake in the suffering of Christ. Many attempt to keep one foot in the world, and the other in Christ, and avoid anything that may result in persecution. Those individuals may not suffer much because they have not made it clear which side they are on, and the enemy may even use them to his advantage. However, if we make it clear to the world, our flesh, and the enemy that we are on God's side, there will be repercussions.

But praise God, *the sufferings of this present time are not worthy to be compared with the coming glory.* This is a true statement. Do you believe it? Do you know that you will be rewarded when you live for Christ, in such a way that you truly won't even recount the things you go through today for the sake of Christ (v. 18)? Keep your eyes on Christ, and don't compromise with the enemy.

19 For the *earnest* hope of the creatures waits for the manifestation of the sons of God.

While we may be called *sons of God* now (v. 16), the *manifestation* of the *sons of God* won't take place until the Lord returns for His people. All that it means to be a son of God will come to fruition later. For now though, we rest in knowing that if we *walk according to the Spirit*, we are indeed *sons of God*, and after this present battle, we will come into a glorious kingdom as *joint-heirs with Christ* (v. 17).

20 For the creatures were subjected to vanity, not willingly, but by reason of him who has subjected them,

> We who are the *sons of God* have been and are being subjected to vanity (this present world), for God's purposes. We may not understand why we need to go through the battles we face and be subjected to the sufferings of life, but we know that this fulfills the *reason of him* who has put us here. Yet we are not without faith, which can move mountains. Fight the battles with courage, and honor Jesus Christ who has fought the same battles, and won.

21 with the hope that the same creatures shall be delivered from the slavery of corruption into the glorious liberty of the sons of God.

> *The hope* is not mere "wishful thinking." This *hope* is real, as we know that the Lord's faithful will indeed be *delivered from the slavery of corruption* and that we will soon be taken *into the glorious liberty*. While here on earth, *hope* burns within us, our hearts, minds, and emotions being filled with expectation for our eternal, *glorious liberty* as *sons of God*.

22 For we *now* know that all the creatures groan *together* and travail in pain *together* until now.

23 And not only they, but ourselves also who have the firstfruits of the Spirit, even we ourselves groan within ourselves, waiting for the adoption, *that is to say*, the redemption of our body.

> If we love the world, we will not care much about *redemption of our body*. But if we walk according to the Spirit, we will *groan within ourselves* while we wait. The pleasures of the world and the pleasures of the flesh might numb the effects of sin and death, but they are temporary and deceiving.

24 For in hope we are saved, but hope that is seen is not hope; for what a man sees, he does not wait for.

25 But if we wait for that which we do not see, with patience we wait for *it*.

> If I have a coffee in my hand, I am presently enjoying the aroma and flavor. But before I hold the coffee in my hands, I am only looking forward in anticipation for it (hope), as I rightly know I will have the coffee in my hand within the hour. This is a dumb example, perhaps, and hardly worth comparing to life and eternity. But the point is, we are presently looking forward to the *redemption of our body* (v. 23), to be fully enjoyed at a later date.

26 ¶ And likewise also the Spirit helps our weakness; for we know not how to pray as we ought, but the Spirit itself makes entreaty for us with groanings which cannot be uttered.

27 But he that searches the hearts knows what is the desire of the Spirit, that according to *the will of* God, he makes entreaty for the saints.

The Spirit does *make entreaty for us*, searching our hearts and praying *according to the will of God*. This is not, as some think, about speaking in tongues. Scripture defines and appropriates speaking in tongues in 1 Corinthians 14, Mark 16, and Acts 2, 10, and 19. This is an important distinction to understand, as speaking in tongues is defined in scripture as a gift of the Spirit, and it is clearly saying here that the *Spirit itself* also makes intercession for us, solely done by the Spirit according to the will of God, for us. These words of the Spirit as described here *cannot be uttered*, and are something that is happening behind the scenes, perhaps even without our being aware when it is happening.

28 And we *now* know that unto those who love God, all things help them unto good, to those who according to the purpose are called *to be saints*.

29 ¶ For *unto* those whom he knew beforehand, he also marked out beforehand that they might be conformed to the image of his Son, that he might be the firstborn among many brethren.

30 And unto those whom he did mark out beforehand, to these he also called; and to whom he called, these he also justified; and to whom he justified, these he also glorified.

31 ¶ What shall we then say to these things? If God *is* for us, who *shall be* against us?

The reality of God's sovereignty (predestination)

regarding those *who are called to be saints* (and *marked out beforehand*) is going to be made very clear in following verses, but what Paul is really addressing right here is the fact that we don't need to fear as we know that *all things help them unto good* if we are *called to be saints* (v. 28). We know that *if God is for us*, no other person can trump His will. We do not need to fear man or even the enemy. We need only fear God. What verse 31 is saying is simply that we can rest in God, who, if He called us out, is certainly *for us* and as such, if the God is for us, who can overcome us (v. 31)?

33 Who shall accuse the chosen of God's? God *is* he that justifies *them*.

34 Who *is* he that condemns *them*? Christ, Jesus, is he who died *and*, even more, he that also rose again, who furthermore is at the right hand of God, who also makes entreaty for us.

35 Who shall separate us from the charity of Christ? *shall* tribulation or distress or persecution or famine or nakedness or peril or sword?

Paul is making it abundantly clear that we don't need to fear *tribulation, distress, persecution, famine, nakedness, peril, or sword*. What are the things you fear as a Christians, the things you think might happen because of your decision to *walk according to the Spirit*? Do you think you might lose your job which may result in you going hungry or not have clothes to wear? Don't worry, even this is no reason to fear. These things indeed may happen, and we ought to be willing for them. But the point here is that these things absolutely, without any doubt, cannot separate us from God. As Christians who *walk according to the Spirit*, our sole desire is to live for Christ and to be redeemed from this body, living instead in eternity with our heavenly Father.

36 (As it is written, For thy sake we are killed all the day long; we are accounted as sheep for the slaughter.)

37 Nevertheless, in all these things we are more than conquerors through him that loved us.

The enemy and the world wants to annihilate us. If we *walk according to the Spirit*, we will indeed suffer in one way or the other. Only rejoice when you are counted worthy to suffer for His name's sake (Acts 5:41).

38 Therefore I am certain that neither death nor life nor angels nor principalities nor powers nor things present nor things to come

39 nor height nor depth nor any creature shall be able to separate us from the charity of God, which is in Christ, Jesus our Lord.

Praise God, there is not a single thing here on earth or in the spiritual world that can separate us from the charity of God.

Notice that the word *charity* is used here. If I receive a charitable contribution, someone is giving an unexpected, undeserved gift to me. It's not even a birthday gift, which is somewhat expected to be received from those we love. But a charitable gift is something solely given at the discretion of the giver, with no expectation from the recipient. And in this case, the unmeasurable gift God is giving us is one that cannot be taken away by anyone other than ourselves. We can return the gift to the Giver, but nobody and no thing can take it away outside of our own refusal to receive it.

Even so, God's own people will not reject the gift. Praise God that He saw fit to reveal that truth to us, so that we may rejoice in this hope we having, knowing that finishing this race is entirely possible as long as we walk *according to the Spirit*, not *according to the flesh*.

Romans 9

1 ¶ I say the truth in Christ, I do not lie, my conscience also bearing me witness in the Holy Spirit,

2 that I have great sorrow and continual pain in my heart.

3 For I could wish that myself were anathema from Christ for my brethren, those who are my kinsmen according to the flesh,

> *I <u>could</u> wish* (v. 3). Paul had *great sorrow and continual pain in* his *heart* (v. 2), for his kinsmen. So sincere was Paul, that if it were practical, or even possible, that he felt as if he might give up his own salvation for the sake of his kinsmen. Did Paul really want to give up his salvation? No, not at all, yet this way of communicating shows the depth of Paul's devotion to his people, and to the ministry that the Lord gave him.

4 who are Israelites, to whom *pertains* the adoption *as* *sons* and the glory and the covenants and the giving of the law and the service *of God* and the promises,

5 whose *are* the fathers, and of whom as concerning the flesh is the Christ, who is God over all things, blessed for all the ages. Amen.

> Paul's kinsmen were Israelites, who were adopted by God as His sons (v. 4), and they were given many blessings and incredible promises. When one is adopted in real life, the one adopted has no means by which to secure his adoption. It is entirely up to the parents to look for a son to adopt in the first place, and as they are searching for a son, it is entirely up to them where they look and whom they choose. As we continue in this chapter, it will become even more evident that Israel didn't choose God, but God chose them.

6 ¶ Not as though the word of God has been deficient. For not all the descendants of Israel are Israelites;

7 neither, because they are the seed of Abraham, are all sons, but, In Isaac shall thy seed be called.

> Not all of Abraham's children were followers of Christ, and Paul makes it clear that this isn't a result of God's promise to Abraham being deficient, but that it is because God's promise to Abraham was only for the children of Isaac.

8 That is, Those who *are* sons of the flesh, these *are* not the sons of God; but those who *are* sons of the promise *are* counted in the generation.

It is not what we do in the flesh that makes us sons of God. Instead, it is him who God calls to be His son (v. 7). Abraham was given the promise, but it was not for all his children, just the children of the promise (Isaac). Of Isaac's children, Jacob was the chosen one, not Esau (v. 13).

Why is this important? There is something bigger going on than we can see with our physical eyes. Much rebellion has taken place in the spiritual realm, even before Adam rebelled. It is necessary to again show exactly who God is. Unless God is in His rightful place as the sovereign one, the current chaos in humanity will only get worse. But through the ages, God has been demonstrating just who He is and we each individually and collectively are merely a small part of that restoration process, for God's purposes and His glory. We are His creation, made alive by God's breath of life, and the not the gods our swollen heads and hearts have led us to believe. All of what God is doing shows how great and how loving He is, despite all the accusations against Him. Eventually, a courtroom-proof case for how great God is will be completed, and it will be sustainable for eternity.

9 For the word of the promise *is* this, At this time I will come, and Sara shall have a son.

10 And not only *this*, but when Rebecca also had conceived by one, *even* by our father Isaac

11 (for *the children* being not yet born, neither having done any good or evil, that the purpose of God according to election might stand: not of works, but of him that calls),

> These verses are so clear that we dare not mess with them. Even if the doctrine of election were only to show up in this one place, we'd still be obligated to believe it because it is so clear. But if something appears again and again in scripture, as this truth does, we'd have to be blind or stubborn to not believe it. Yet few read these words of scripture here and believe them.

> But if you believe that the scripture is true, then you must believe that verse 11 is true. You may want to go back and read the verse again, and be sure to simply let the words say what they say. Let all apparently opposing scripture say what it says too, and simply and strictly believe that all reconciles in the end. To reconcile, one thing doesn't cancel the other out. Instead, both sides have their place, and both are necessary. Here Paul is speaking about things from God's perspective, and all scripture that talks about our responsibility is talking about man's perspective. Yet, we know both sides are 100% true. It's not a meeting in the middle of both sides, but 100% and 100% true, and the two are to be reconciled, not added together.

12 it was said unto her, The elder shall serve the younger.

> So clear did it need to be that God is the one who does the calling that He even chose the younger, a

direct reversal of what was the norm and a clear indication that God gets to choose as He will.

13 As it is written, Jacob have I loved, but Esau have I hated.

Barely can we get ourselves to acknowledge that God is capable of hate. It's not, however, because we as humans are so loving that we think God cannot hate. Rather, it is because we want to do whatever we want to do, and wish to think that God will love us regardless. That is not the case, and we are far underestimating who God is. God is powerful and almighty and to be feared. He is also loving, but on His terms, not ours. There's a reason for this, as well soon see.

14 ¶ What shall we say then? *Is there* injustice in God? No, in no wise.

It is of utmost importance to realize that there is no injustice in God. God is not unfair, He is a just God.

15 For he saith to Moses, I will have mercy on whom I will have mercy, and I will have compassion on whom I will have compassion.

16 So then *it is* not of him that wills, nor of him that runs, but of God that has mercy.

As this narrative unfolds, keep watching the words. A solid, secure case for the sovereignty of God is being built, a narrative that once our eyes are open we can see throughout all of scripture. Here, in these two verses, everything comes together in perhaps the most easy-to-understand picture of what God's sovereignty is and why it exists. It is also of utmost importance to understand God's position in this, which will reveal that God is an awesome, wonderful, and loving God.

17 For the scripture saith of Pharaoh, Even for this same purpose have I raised thee up, that I might show my power in thee and that my name might be declared throughout all the earth.

18 Therefore he has mercy on whom he will *have mercy*, and he hardens whom he will.

We sometimes look at men and are amazed at all the good or all the evil that they are doing, and given them all the credit or blame. Yet the reality is that they are only serving the purposes of God. He has raised up each one of us for His purposes – it was and is necessary that everything that is happening does happen in order to *show His power* and to *declare His name throughout all the earth. Woe unto the world because of offenses! For it must needs be that offenses come, but woe to that man by whom the offense comes!* (Matthew 18:7)

Is it unnerving to know that you didn't chose God and that you are at His mercy? You didn't have the power to initiate your conception, and you certainly don't have the power to sustain your life. You are a sinner to the core, yet you think there is enough good in you, enough power in you, so that you can choose God? This is the same God whom you can't even look at face to face without dying, yet you think you will seek Him out and that you will decide to serve Him, all on your own initiative? Impossible. *No one can come to me* [Jesus] *unless the Father who has sent me draws him* (John 6:44a).

19 Thou wilt say then unto me, Why does he become angry? For who shall resist his will?

20 Rather, O man, who art thou to reply against God? Shall the thing formed say to him that formed *it*, Why hast thou made me thus?

21 Has not the potter power over the clay, of the same lump to make one vessel unto honour and another unto dishonour?

> We are God's creation, not our own. If you bake a cake, do you not have the power to make one a brown cake, and another a white cake? You certainly don't question your ability and reasoning behind doing so, but you do what you will for your own use and purposes. Likewise, we are here by God and for God, for His use and purposes, not for our own. *Who shall resist his will?* (v. 19) No one.

22 *What* if God, desiring to show *his* wrath and to make his power known, endured with much meekness the vessels of wrath, prepared for death,

23 and making known the riches of his glory on the vessels of mercy, which he has prepared unto glory?

The purpose of God is defined by these two truths: 1) God is showing His wrath and making His power known through "vessels of dishonor", and 2) God is making known the riches of His glory on "vessels of honor."

It's interesting to note that while verse 21 distinguishes the two types of created mankind as either vessels of honor, or vessels of dishonor, yet in verse 23 He actually calls vessels of honor "vessels of mercy." This fits with verses 15 through 18, which are all about how God shows mercy to His chosen ones, making it clear that is Him showing *mercy* that counts for anything. It's got nothing to do with us, but with the Creator, for His purposes, and us simply being clay in the potter's hand.

24 Even us, whom he has called, not of the Jews only, but also of the Gentiles!

25 ¶ As he saith also in Hosea, I will call them my people, who were not my people, and her beloved, who was not beloved.

26 And it shall come to pass *that* in the place where it was said unto them, Ye *are* not my people, there shall they be called sons of the living God.

To make it even clearer that He is the one who calls people to Himself, God first set apart a chosen son (Israel), out of which He chose Jacob, God then even calls individuals out of the unchosen Gentiles, and even calls out some individuals from the children of Ishmael. This all shows even more of God's sovereignty.

In the United States of America, any citizen has the privilege to run for public office. But even in this free country, it is not possible for a citizen from another country to run for public office in our country. In electing Gentiles, God is making it clear that He knows no bounds, and at the same time, it is He who specifically and according to His own will calls people to Himself, for His purposes.

27 Isaiah also cries out concerning Israel, Though the number of the sons of Israel be as the sand of the sea, only a remnant shall be saved;

Paul is quoting from Isaiah 10:22-23. It's clear from reading these scriptures that many are called, but few are chosen (Matthew 22:14). Even though the seed of Israel was called, out of all Israel's children only a remnant is saved. How that reconciles with what we just read earlier in this chapter may seem like a mystery, but what we see here if we look closely is that God rejects some, calls some, and choses some. This may seem like a mystery to us, but we can rest assured that it is not a mystery to God, and that all is working together according to His purposes and for His glory.

28 when the consumption comes to an end, righteousness shall overflow, because a short sentence will the Lord execute upon the earth.

In the end, *righteousness shall overflow.* The Lord is going to *execute a short sentence upon the earth,* but in his mercy, this is a *short* sentence. It's necessary that there is a judgement for the earth, but it is not going to be very long relative to how long the whole earth has been in rebellion against God. This is not talking about hell, the worst of possible punishments, but likely of the tribulation on earth.

29 And as Isaiah said before, Except the Lord of the hosts had left us a seed, we had been as Sodom and been made like unto Gomorrha.

30 ¶ What shall we say then? That the Gentiles, who did not follow after righteousness, have attained to righteousness, that is to say, the righteousness which is by faith,

31 and Israel, which followed after the law of righteousness, has not attained to the law of righteousness.

32 Why? Because *they followed it* not by faith but, as it were, by the works (of the law); therefore, they stumbled on the stumblingstone;

33 as it is written, Behold, I lay in Sion a stumblingstone and rock *that will cause some* to fall, and whosoever believes in him shall not be ashamed.

> Mid-chapter, Paul switches to man's responsibility. Of course, the scriptures were not originally broken into chapters. This causes some confusion though, as many people read these later verses and

can't figure out how to reconcile what is in the latter part of chapter 9 with the earlier part of chapter 9.

Paul is addressing both God's sovereignty and man's responsibility in this part of Romans. But God, through the writers of the Bible, was very efficient with His words and often many topics are addressed in each book of the Bible.

Verse 32 makes it clear that both the Jew and the Gentile is justified by faith. We *obtained to righteousness* (v. 30) not by works, but by faith. We are drawn to the Father not because we seek Him, but because He seeks us (John 6:44). This passage has been a thorough and balanced passage, and is even more so when all of Romans is weighed as a whole. The Bible is a complete, comprehensive book, far different from books written by man which may cover one main point, and that often in an imbalanced way.

Romans 10

1 ¶ Brethren, certainly the desire of my heart and my prayer to God regarding Israel, is for saving health.

> Paul is definitely not a Jonah. Most of us likely sometimes doubt that individuals or a nation can repent, and sometimes we even don't want them to do so. But as much as the Jews persecuted Paul, and as much reason as he had to disregard them as candidates for salvation, the desire of his heart was still that they be saved. He had a real heart of love for his people.

2 For I give testimony that they have a zeal of God, but not according to knowledge.

3 For they, being ignorant of God's righteousness and going about to establish their own righteousness, have not submitted themselves unto the righteousness of God.

4 For Christ *is* the end of the law, to *give* righteousness to every one that believes.

> The Jews had *a zeal for* God, but Paul's desire was that the Jews submit to the righteousness that is of God (v. 2-3). This righteousness is Christ, which is given *to every one that believes in Him* (v. 4). Paul preached an uncompromising message of salvation by faith and of the necessity of living according to the Spirit rather than the flesh (Romans 8:13). There was not a touch of "social gospel" or "God-is-only-love" or any other off-balanced teaching that we find coming from too many pulpits today. Paul preached the righteousness of Jesus Christ, and the importance of living a life for Him.

5 For Moses describes the righteousness which is by the law, That the man who does those things shall live by them.

6 But thus saith the righteousness which is by faith, Say not in thine heart, Who shall ascend into heaven (that is, to bring the Christ down *from above*)?

7 Or, Who shall descend into the deep (that is, to bring up the Christ again from the dead)?

> We cannot ourselves duplicate what Christ has done, neither does Christ need to die on the cross again for those who sinned since. Rather, Christ died once for all (Romans 6:10). As such, Christ is the fulfillment of the law, and if we are in Him, our faith is counted as our righteousness.

If we attempt to obtain righteousness by the law of Moses (v. 5), we are simply living by the law. But we need Christ, and the Levitical sacrificial system was fulfilled in Christ, who was the sacrifice that ended the need for any future sacrifices. We now obtain forgiveness of sins and removal of guilt through His blood.

8 But what does it say? The word is near thee, *even* in thy mouth and in thy heart: that is, the word of faith, which we preach,

9 that if thou shalt confess with thy mouth the Lord Jesus and shalt believe in thine heart that God has raised him from the dead, thou shalt be saved.

10 For with the heart one believes unto righteousness, and with the mouth confession is made unto saving health.

> Believe with *thy heart.* Our heart is the center of our being and where the Spirit of the Lord dwells. Perhaps not literally in our heart (this is somewhat vague in scripture), but certainly in the general vicinity of our heart. Some mistakenly think the Holy Spirit resides in our head, but this is definitely not according to scripture. It is important to realize that the heart is where issues of life, or death, flow from.
>
> If we confess with our mouth, we are fulfilling what Jesus said: The good man out of the good treasure of his heart brings forth that which is good, and the evil man out of the evil treasure of his heart brings forth that which is evil, for of the abundance of the heart his mouth speaks (Luke 6:45).
>
> It isn't what goes into our mouth that defiles us,

but what comes out of our mouth that shows what is in our heart (Matthew 15:17-20). If our heart is evil, evil things will come out of our mouth. If our heart is good (and it can only be good if the Lord touches it) then good things will come out of our mouth. It is also for this reason that the greatest commandment starts by saying we must love God with all our <u>heart</u>: *Thou shalt love the Lord thy God with all thy <u>heart</u>...* (Luke 10:27).

11 For the scripture says, Whosoever believes on him shall not be ashamed.

Paul is referring to Isaiah 45:17. The verse right before that says *all the makers of idols shall go forth ashamed*. Why will *makers of idols* be ashamed? Because not only do they have a false religion, but also because worshipping and praying to idols made of rocks or wood is laughable. The same, it would be laughable if we were found worshipping and praying to an invisible God who ends up being false. But, we *shall <u>not</u> be ashamed*. We have this confidence in biblical, extra-biblical, and personal experiential verification of what is true, and those who love and worship the Lord will not be in the least ashamed in the end. We will not be ashamed.

12 ¶ For there is no difference between the Jew and the Greek, for the same Lord over all is rich unto all that call upon him.

13 For whosoever shall call upon the name of the Lord shall be saved.

As a Gentile personally, I do not need to worry about being ashamed in the end, having placed my faith in the Lord Jesus Christ even though He came first and foremost to the lost sheep of the house of Israel (Matthew 15:24). Praise the Lord, the door was opened to all who *call upon the name of the Lord*, including me and you. Praise the Lord, I do not need to be ashamed in the end for having placed my faith in something unobtainable.

14 How then shall they call on him in whom they have not believed? and how shall they believe him of whom they have not heard? and how shall they hear without a preacher?

15 And how shall they preach if they have not been sent? as it is written, How beautiful *are* the feet of those that announce the gospel of peace, of those that announce the gospel of that which is good!

The truth needs to be preached. If those whom God calls to preach don't do so, then the people won't hear. The Gospel of Jesus Christ must be preached to the whole world (Matthew 24:14), and God has chosen to work through men to do this.

This Gospel is the Lord's however, and it is His word alone through His chosen preachers alone who can do this wonderful work. *How beautiful are the feet* of those who preach the unadulterated, undiluted, and full counsel of the *Gospel of peace*. The men who are entertaining their audiences, who are bending to the political themes of the day, or who are teaching their people that it is normal to continue in sin – these men are not the chosen of God, or at the least they are not obedient to God.

16 But not everyone hearkens unto the gospel. For Isaiah says, Lord, who has believed our report?

17 So then faith *comes* by hearing, and *the* ear *to hear* by the word of God.

> Not only must the preachers be chosen and sent by God, but the hearers must also hear the word of God. Meaning, the fault lies as much with the hearers as with the preachers for our current lukewarm and cold Christian climate.

> I have many times and in various ways asked the Lord to open my heart to the truth, and it is a simple necessity to do so, and to continue doing so. There is no teacher greater than the Spirit of God, and if we are sincere, He will teach us directly, as well as through preachers of the Word. Ask Him to touch you and make you pliable clay in His hands, to bend your will to meet His will.

18 But I say, Have they not heard? Yes verily, their fame went into all the earth, and their words unto the ends of the world.

19 But I say, Did not Israel know? First Moses says, I will provoke you unto jealousy with people that are not mine, *and* with ignorant people I will provoke you to anger.

All of Israel heard the true Gospel, but it didn't go further than their ears. As a result, the Lord turned to the Gentiles. Gentiles were untaught in the things of God, not having been given the law or the promises of God. But God also called *ignorant people* in order to provoke *Israel* to *anger.*

20 But Isaiah is very bold and says, I was found by those that did not seek me; I manifested myself unto those that did not ask after me.

21 And against Israel he says, All day long I have stretched forth my hands unto a disobedient and gainsaying people.

By this, the Lord reached out to both Jew and Gentile and made His grace known to mankind. He *manifested* himself *unto those who did not ask after* Him, and He also *stretched forth* His *hands unto a disobedient and gainsaying people* (Israel, who rebelled even though they did know the truth).

Romans 11

1 ¶ I say then, Has God cast away his people? No, in no wise. For I also am an Israelite, of the seed of Abraham, *of* the tribe of Benjamin.

> The proof that God has not cast away His chosen people, the Israelites, is evident even in Paul himself, a Jew called by God. Paul was clearly called by God on the road to Damascas, in no way seeking God himself. In fact, Paul was only out to persecute other Christians when the Lord stopped him in his tracks, spoke to him, and opened his eyes to the truth.

2 God has not cast away his people whom he knew beforehand. Know ye not what the scripture says of Elijah? how speaking to God against Israel, he said,

> God, through Paul, is reiterating that even though much of Israel was disobedient, the fact remains that God didn't reject His chosen people, despite their rebellion. There is a remnant chosen by God, elected and saved for His purposes.

3 Lord, they have killed thy prophets and ruined thine altars; and I am left alone, and they seek my life.

4 But what did the answer of God say unto him? I have reserved to myself seven thousand men, who have not bowed the knee before Baal.

5 Even so then at this present time also, there is a remnant by the gracious election *of God*.

> Elijah felt all alone, and it really appeared that was the case (v. 2-4). The enemy had killed the prophets and ruined the altars (v. 3). Do you feel alone? Do you feel as if the enemy has silenced all of God's true servants and ruined our churches? Don't worry, there is still a remnant preserved by God. He knows where they are, and if you ask, He will surely direct you to His people for wonderful, genuine fellowship and brotherhood.

6 And if by grace, then *is it* not by works; otherwise, the grace is no longer grace. But if *it is* of works, then it is no longer grace; otherwise, the work is no longer work.

> This elect group of people are saved not because of how good they are, but are redeemed by the grace of God, through Jesus Christ. The Lord didn't leave it up to people to remember all that has previously been said about salvation by grace, but reiterated it here too, leaving no room to think that the elect has been saved in any way outside of grace.

7 What then? Israel has not obtained that which he

seeks after; but the elect have obtained it, and the rest were blinded

8 (according as it is written, God has given them the spirit of anguish, eyes with which they do not see and ears with which they do not hear) unto this day.

> *The elect have obtained it, and the rest were blinded* (v. 7). This theme of Israel being blinded will be clarified as we continue in Romans. And it is *unto this day* (v. 8) as well. Israel as a whole is still blinded, though there is indeed a remnant that does serve God.

9 And David says, Let their table be turned into a snare and a net and a stumblingblock and a recompense unto them;

10 Let their eyes be darkened that they may not see, and bow down their back always.

> That this would happen was prophesied by King David (v. 9). This is also a warning to Gentiles, as God will not permit wickedness to continue. Eventually the wicked ones, and even wicked nations as a whole, will be given over to a reprobate mind (Romans 1:28).

11 I say then, Have they stumbled in such a manner that they should fall completely? No, in no wise; but *rather* through their fall, saving health *is come* unto the Gentiles to provoke them unto jealousy.

> The purpose for the "fall" of Israel is clearly presented as being for the salvation of the Gentiles.

How and why Israel had to be hardened in order for the Gentiles to be saved is a bit of a mystery. Yet we know that this is true since scripture clearly presents this to be true. We do know, however, that all things work together for God's purposes and for His glory.

12 And if the fall of them is the riches of the world, and the diminishing of them the riches of the Gentiles, how much more *shall* their fullness *be*?

But praise the Lord, there is a coming *fullness* through which Israel will be forgiven, for the sake of their fathers (Romans 11:28). Also important to note here is that God enclosed all in disobedience, that he might have mercy on all (Romans 11:32). By everyone's disobedience, an even stronger case for God's mercy is made.

13 For (I call you Gentiles) inasmuch as I am truly the apostle of the Gentiles, my honorable ministry,

14 if in any manner I may provoke my nation to jealousy and cause some of them to be saved.

Paul understood the plan of God intimately. Instead of becoming bitter towards the Jews, who rejected his ministry, Paul went to the Gentiles with the Gospel of Christ, realizing that as the Gentiles came to Christ, the Jews would be *provoked to jealousy*, according to the plan of God.

15 For if the casting away of them is the reconciling of the world, what *shall* the receiving *of them be*, but life from the dead?

The reason Israel had their eyes darkened (v. 10) was so the rest of the world might be saved. That being the reason, how much more will the mercy of God be for their restoration (*life from the dead*). What a mighty God we serve, and what an intricate, beautiful plan He has, which will show forth His glory and display His mercy to mankind.

16 For if the firstfruit is holy, so *shall* the rest be; and if the root *is* holy, so *shall be* the branches.

17 And if some of the branches were broken off, and thou, being a wild olive tree, wert grafted in among them and hath been made participant of the root and of the fatness of the olive tree,

18 do not boast against the branches. But if thou boast, *know* that thou dost not bear the root, but the root thee.

We as Gentiles are merely grafted into the true olive tree, which is Israel (Jeremiah 11:16). Sadly, many *wild olive trees* (Gentile Christians) are boasting against the branches, many even claiming that they are the new Israel, and that God's plan for Israel as the chosen people has ceased. This is a foolish assumption, and these people have obviously not read this scripture - or if they have, their arrogance has blinded their understanding.

19 Thou wilt say then, The branches were broken off that I might be grafted in.

20 Good; because of *their* unbelief they were broken

off, but thou by faith art standing. Do not be highminded, but fear

21 that if God did not forgive the natural branches, neither shall he forgive thee.

> Even when this was written, some Gentiles were saying that God *broke off* Israel, so that the Gentiles *might be grafted in* (v. 19). But Paul says that we are merely standing by faith. We ought to fear, because if God didn't forgive the natural branches for their rebellion, how much less will He forgive branches that are merely grafted in? We must be careful lest we be found dry and lacking any true olive fruit, or we *wild olive branches* may well be cut off and thrown into the fire.

22 Behold, therefore, the goodness and severity of God: on those who fell, severity, but toward thee, goodness if thou continue in *his* goodness; otherwise thou also shalt be cut off.

> This verse strikes a blow at the once-saved-always-saved theory. It is certainly possible to not *continue in his goodness*, and if that is the case, we will *be cut off*. This is cause for carefulness and sincerity towards God. Sloppy, shallow Christianity is not only embarrassing, it is also dangerous. God does not need to forgive our sins, nor will He continually do so. There is a point where we risk being cut off. How close we Gentiles as a whole are to this, I do not know. But I do know we're treading dangerously close to that borderline.

23 And even them, if they do not continue in unbelief, shall be grafted in, for God is powerful *enough* to graft them in again.

24 For if thou wert cut out of the olive tree *which is* wild by nature and wert grafted contrary to nature into the good olive tree, how much more shall these, which are the natural *branches*, be grafted into their own olive tree?

> God is ready and willing to graft the natural branches (Israel) back into the tree. Will they *continue in unbelief* (v. 23)? It seems that they will not continue in unbelief forever (v. 26-29).

25 For I would not, brethren, that ye ignore this mystery, that ye not be arrogant regarding yourselves: that blindness in part has happened in Israel, until the fullness of the Gentiles are come in.

> This is a *mystery*, yet Paul says we should not be ignorant of it. We may not understand all of what is behind this truth, but it is made plain enough that we can read and understand what is being said. We may not understand the *why*, but we certainly can understand the *what*.

> Israel has been blinded *in part*, until all the Gentiles who are chosen of the Lord are *come in*.

26 And even if all Israel were saved, as it is written: There shall come out of Sion the Deliverer, and shall take away the ungodliness from Jacob;

27 and this shall be my covenant unto them when I shall take away their sins.

28 So that, as concerning the gospel, *I have them for* enemies for your sakes; but as touching the election *of God*, they are beloved for the fathers' sakes.

29 For the gifts and calling of God are without repentance.

> Israel is *beloved* for the sake of their fathers (v. 28). The promises to their fathers will not be broken (v. 29), and Israel will be saved. All we need to do is read the Old Testament, and we will see promise after promise of life for Israel. God chose them despite their disobedience, and He will keep His promises.
>
> V. 29 is sometimes mistakenly used to attempt to prove that we cannot lose our salvation, or that if we're given a spiritual gift, that it won't be taken away, regardless of what we do. This is not the context here, however. We certainly may have spiritual gifts taken away from us, and we certainly may lose our salvation. These things are verified in other scriptures (such as 2 Peter 2:20-22, and Hebrews 6:4-6).

30 For as ye in time past have not obeyed God, yet have now obtained mercy through the occasion of their disobedience,

> We as Gentiles cannot claim that God had mercy on us because of us first being obedient. Instead, we *have obtained mercy* and that only through the *occasion of their disobedience*. This makes us

indebted to the Jews, and we ought to have mercy towards them.

The fact that the United States of America has stood as a friend to Israel may be the only reason God is still holding out His scepter towards our nation, both for the salvation of our people as well as the reason for our being blessed in so many ways. Turning our back on the nation of Israel would surely be a mistake, in light of the scripture we're reading. This is not a political statement, but a spiritual statement. So much has been given to Israel, and he who blesses Israel will be blessed (Genesis 12:3).

31 likewise these also have not believed now that through the mercy shown unto you they also may obtain mercy.

32 For God enclosed everyone in disobedience, that he might have mercy upon everyone.

Mercy is only shown to people who need it – it isn't mercy if given to those who have no need. Being *enclosed in disobedience* is grounds for receiving mercy. Why it's revealed to us that God <u>enclosed *everyone in disobedience*</u> can only be speculated, but the fact remains that He is the one who did it. All we can do is believe that what He says through scripture is true, allowing Him the right to do as He sees best, and following through with obedience to the things He asks us to do.

33 ¶ O the depth of the riches both of the wisdom and

of the knowledge of God! How incomprehensible are his judgments and his ways past finding out!

34 For who has understood the intent of the Lord? or who has been his counsellor?

35 Or who has first given unto him, that it be recompensed unto him again?

> Truly, *How incomprehensible are his judgments and his ways past finding out!* Who can understand the ways and the purposes of God? We see from reading this passage what God is doing, and we can rest assured that what He is doing is good. And as we allow God to lead us and to direct us, we will be the blessed recipients of His benefits.

36 For of him and by him and in him *are* all things. To him *be* the glory for *the* ages. Amen.

Romans 12

1 ¶ Therefore, I beseech you brethren, by the mercies of God, that ye present your bodies in living sacrifice, holy, well pleasing unto God, *which is* your rational worship.

It is our reasonable service to present our bodies (our life) as a *living sacrifice, holy, well pleasing to God*. It is not unreasonable, as some seem to think, that God expects us to live lives that are honoring to Him. In any capacity of employment, from the position of a CEO, to the janitor, the individual must represent the company he is working for in a good light. Surely it is reasonable that we must do the same God, the same God who was merciful to us and sent His undeserving son to take our place on the cross, and who is Himself holy and perfect.

2 And be not conformed to this age, but be ye transformed by the renewing of your soul that ye may experience what *is* that good and well pleasing and perfect will of God.

There is a prevalent belief in the church that we must accommodate the world in order to win the world. This has affected everything from how we dress, to the music that is performed, to how the message is delivered in the church. In the private life of Christians, many still watch the world's movies, listened to the world's music, and join in the festivities of the world. What is done for pleasure, or in the name of reaching the world, must be reexamined in light of this verse.

3 Therefore I say through the grace given unto me, to all those that are among you not to obtain more knowledge than is prudent to know, but to obtain knowledge with temperance, each one according to the measure of faith that God has dealt.

4 For in the manner that we have many members in one body, nevertheless all the members do not have the same operation;

This is a timely caution to not constantly be pursing knowledge (v. 3) or even to try to fulfill all roles within the church ourselves. This, however, has not to do with worldly knowledge necessarily, but regarding spiritual knowledge (v. 4). The body of Christ has many members, many faculties and gifts, and works best together with others in the body. Some Christians do nothing except read books and watch videos on all spiritual subjects, rather than simply fulfilling the gifts and spiritual roles that the Lord has ordained them to do.

5 likewise many of us are one body in Christ, and every one members one of another.

6 So that having different gifts according to the grace that is given to us, whether prophecy, according to the measure of faith;

7 or ministry, in serving; or he that teaches, in doctrine;

8 he that exhorts, in exhortation; he that gives, *let him do it* in simplicity; he that presides, in earnest care; he that shows mercy, in cheerfulness.

> The lines in these gifts have not only been blurred, they are often not even recognized. We ought to do whatever we've been given to do with all our heart, *according to the grace that is given to us* for that particular ministry. As we fulfill our roles well and with good hearts, the Lord may give us other, "more important" roles or perhaps just expand our current roles into larger settings. What matters is that we do well and for the Lord's glory the things we've been called to do.

9 *Let* love be without dissimulation, abhorring that which is evil, causing you to come unto that which is good;

10 loving one another with brotherly love, with honour preferring one another;

> It's interesting that love is connected to *abhorring evil* here (v. 9). Love should be in the form that it causes us *to come unto that which is good*. And brothers and sisters in Christ, those who love good and abhor

evil, we should love one another with brotherly love (which is genuine and deep), so much so that we esteem others better than ourselves (Philippians 2:3).

In order to abhor that which is evil, we must love the Lord above all else. It's only when we genuinely come in contact with the Lord and He renews a right spirit within us, that we are able to understand the things He loves as well as the things He hates. Likewise, it is only when we deny ourselves and follow Christ that we can love our brothers and sisters as we ought. Only by denying the flesh and walking according to the Spirit (Romans 8).

11 not slothful in earnest care, *but* fervent in *the* Spirit, serving the Lord,

We are to be as ready as military personal might be ready to fight, serving the Lord day and night, mobilized at moment's notice.

12 rejoicing in hope, patient in tribulation, constant in prayer,

Constant in prayer doesn't mean praying every single minute of every day, but it does mean that we take every need to the Lord in prayer, both for ourselves and others in need. The praying we ought to do is not a quick prayer breathed to heaven with barely a thought, but it is a sincere prayer to our Holy God.

13 sharing for the needs of the saints, *and* given to hospitality.

Christians of today tend to give money to the church, which is then used to pay the pastors and pay for the building and church programs. Outside of regular giving to the church, individuals might fund ministries of choice, and perhaps give money to family and close friends as needed.

The mandate here, however, looks a bit different. We are to share the needs of *all* saints, and be given to hospitality of all saints. Suppose churches, instead of primarily funneling the majority of funds towards pastors' salaries and buildings, we also distributed funds to meet the needs of the saints. Widows who are widows indeed would be provided for (1 Timothy 5:3-16), as would the fatherless and those who genuinely need our help.

14 Bless those who persecute you: bless, and do not curse.

To have a heart that is right towards those who curse us takes a heart that is soft and tender, and first and foremost towards God. Our natural tendencies are to curse those who hurt us, or to write them off as our permanent enemies. This does not mean that we need to remain best friends with our enemies (Matthew 18:15-17), but it does mean that we do not return evil for evil, but good for evil.

15 Rejoice with those that rejoice and weep with those that weep.

True Christian love is not envious, and our heart should genuinely and enthusiastically rejoice in the

Lord with those who rejoice in the Lord. Likewise, when saints weep, Paul tells us to weep with them. Here he does not say that we should offer them advice, console them, or take them to a counsellor, though there is nothing necessarily wrong with those things. But if we weep with those who weep, it is a real way we can bear one another's burdens.

16 *Be* unanimous among yourselves, not high minded, but accommodating the humble. Do not be wise in your *own* opinion.

> *Do not be wise in your own opinion.* The truth is, most of us have opinions about everything, and we usually take our opinions to be rock-solid truth.

17 Not repaying anyone evil for evil; procuring that which is good not only in the sight of God, but even in the sight of all men.

18 If it can be done, as much as *is possible* on your part, live in peace with all men.

> What Paul is saying here seems to contradict with what Jesus said in Matthew 10:34: *Think not that I have come to introduce peace into the land; I came not to introduce peace, but a sword.* However, what Paul is saying here is that *as much as is possible,* we are to live in peace. Living in peace is not the main goal, but it is a desired outcome. Unfortunately, many Christians try to make peace with enemies of the gospel, even to the point of compromising truth for the sake of "peace," yet they do not live in

peace with those who they really ought to be living in peace with.

19 Not defending yourselves, dearly beloved; but rather give place unto the wrath *of God*, for it is written, Vengeance *is* mine; I will repay, saith the Lord.

It is clear that the Lord is the one who will get vengeance. Anything done against us because of our position in the Lord will also be avenged by the Lord. Assuming we are really in the Lord, anything done against us is not really against us, but against the Lord. Vengeance is His to take, not ours. It is not our honor and dignity that is being attacked, but the Lord's.

20 Therefore, if thine enemy hungers, feed him; if he thirsts, give him drink; for in so doing thou shalt heap coals of fire on his head.

21 Do not be overcome by evil, but overcome evil with good.

Our job is to *overcome evil with good*. What a commandment, and what a lifestyle we are called to live. No longer our own, we care no longer for our own honor and dignity, but desire only to see the Lord Jesus Christ honored and dignified, even if this means we must do the impossible by being kind to those who misuse and even persecute us. This is a simple commandment, but sometimes not-so-simple to execute. Only if we truly deny ourselves are we able to carry this out. But praise the Lord, we can do this with His help, and further honor the One who was also unjustly treated, for our sake.

Romans 13

1 ¶ Let every soul submit itself to the higher powers. For there is no power but of God, and the powers that be are ordained of God.

2 Whosoever therefore resists the power, resists the ordinance of God, and those that resist shall receive condemnation to themselves.

> If this were not in scripture, we might think that we are above the law of the land. But we Christians are not to be known for breaking the law, at least not unless our nation's laws directly contradict God's law. We are to be known for good, not for evil.

3 For the magistrates are not a terror unto those who do good, but to the *doer of* evil. Is thy desire therefore to not fear the power? do that which is good, and thou shalt have praise of the same;

> It is a little embarrassing that this had to be written to the Romans, and it is just as embarrassing that

we need to hear this today. Christians ought to be known for doing good, not for doing evil. But today, how many lawsuits are initiated by Christians, how many use drink or illegal drugs, and how many cheat on taxes? How many who are in prisons claim to be Christians? It is indeed embarrassing that we have to again tell our brothers and sisters that they must obey the law.

4 for he is *a* minister of God for thy good. But if thou do that which is evil, be afraid; for he does not bear the sword in vain, for he is *a* minister of God, a revenger to *execute* wrath upon him that does evil.

5 Therefore it is necessary that *ye* be subject, not only for punishment, but also for conscience sake.

We should obey our ruling authorities as much as is biblically possible, not only to avoid punishment, but for the sake of a clean conscience. It is one thing if a child obeys to avoid being punished by his parents, but much better if he obeys out of love and inward motivation.

6 For this cause ye also pay *them* tribute, for they are God's ministers, attending continually to this very thing.

7 ¶ Render therefore to all their dues: tribute to whom tribute *is due*; custom to whom custom; fear to whom fear; honour to whom honour.

If taxes are due, we are to pay the taxes unbegrudgingly. It's interesting that Paul mentions fearing those to whom fear is due. No doubt this is not about being scared of men, but a healthy level of respect. Likewise, we should honor those whom are worthy of honor. We are to willingly pay taxes for the support of those who have the rule over us.

8 Owe no one anything, but love one unto another; for he that loves *his* neighbour has fulfilled the law.

9 For this, Thou shalt not commit adultery, Thou shalt not murder, Thou shalt not steal, Thou shalt not bear false witness, Thou shalt not covet, and if *there is* any other commandment, it is briefly comprehended in this saying, namely, Thou shalt love thy neighbour as thyself.

10 Charity works no evil to a neighbour; therefore, charity is the fulfillment of the law.

> If we truly love one another, we will not hurt them in any way, nor will we owe them anything, choosing rather to serve them. The commandment is to not owe them anything to begin with (v. 8). We would avoid so many problems if we only managed to avoid situations that incur debt to others to begin with (and this is not talking about monetary debt only).

11 ¶ And this, knowing the time, that now *it is* high time to awaken ourselves out of sleep, for now *is* our saving health nearer than when we believed.

> While we may be saved, the completion of what was begun is yet to be seen. That day is fast approaching, and if we knew just how close it would be, we'd feel a sense of urgency to set our arrears in order, in both a natural and spiritual sense.

12 The night is past, and the day is come; let us therefore cast off the works of darkness, and let us clothe ourselves *with* the weapons of light.

13 Let us walk honestly, as in the day, not in rioting and drunkenness, not in chambering and wantonness, not in strife and envying.

> Paul is making a straightforward petition to the reader to stop with all *works of darkness*, walking *honestly* as we do during the day. Most sin and crimes are committed at night, in the dark. But Mark 4:22 says *there is nothing hid which shall not be manifested; nor secret which shall not be exposed*. It's far better to *cast off the works of darkness* now, than to wait until everything is exposed in the end, against our will.

14 But *be* clothed *with* the Lord Jesus Christ, and do not listen to the flesh, to *fulfil* its desires.

> The desires of the flesh are never good, and we are told to *not listen to the flesh*. Instead, *be clothed with the Lord Jesus Christ*, which will result in us walking according to the Spirit. We are being prepared for that great and glorious day, and all pain of achieving that today will be rewarded beyond comparison tomorrow.

Romans 14

1 ¶ Bear *with* the one who is sick in the faith, *but* not unto doubtful discernment.

2 For one believes that he may eat all things; another, who is sick, eats vegetables.

> It would take one who is quite weak in faith to think he should only eat vegetables. Yet Paul says to bear with him, even though our tendency may be to look down on that individual, or perhaps even try to correct them, and often so in a condescending manner. But, Paul does add that we should not embrace the thinking for ourselves (v. 1b). *Bearing with him* carries the idea that we extend as much patience as is needed towards our weaker brothers and sisters, while still staying strong in faith ourselves.

3 Let not him that eats despise him that does not eat, and let not him who does not eat judge him that eats; for God has raised him up.

4 Who art thou that judgest another man's servant? By his *own* master he stands or falls; and *if he falls*, he shall be made to stand, for God is powerful to make him stand.

> Paul is making it clear that we should not worry about the little, unimportant differences we see in others, instead having love that is larger than the unimportant differences in weaker members. Paul is not talking about accepting heresy, but simply about things that are neither here nor there. If a person's heart is towards God, *God is powerful to make him stand* (v.4).

5 Also, some make a difference between one day and another; others esteem every day *alike*. Let each one be fully persuaded in his own soul.

6 He that observes the day, let him observe it unto the Lord; and he that does not observe the day, to the Lord he does not observe *it*. He that eats, eats unto the Lord, for he gives God thanks; and he that does not eat, unto the Lord he does not eat, and gives God thanks.

> Whatever we do, we must do it *unto the Lord*. Our heart (motives) often determine whether or not something is wrong. And if our heart is genuinely towards the Lord, not towards ourselves or the world, then we can hardly go wrong. As such, assuming we are doing whatever we are doing *unto the Lord*, let us simply be *persuaded in <u>our own</u> soul*, and let us give *God thanks*.

7 For none of us live for ourselves, and no one dies for himself.

8 For if we live, we live for the Lord; and if we die, we die for the Lord; whether we live therefore, or die, we are the Lord's.

9 For to this end Christ both died and rose *and revived*: to thus exercise lordship over the dead as well as over the living.

> We are *the Lord's*, if we are in Christ. Even those who are "dead" are the Lord's, if they are in Christ. Those who are "alive" in Christ are the Lord's. It is impossible to be in Christ and not be the Lord's. This is a relief, given all the confusion and schisms we see in the church over what is in reality only little, unimportant differences.

10 But why dost thou judge thy brother? or why dost thou belittle thy brother? for we shall all stand before the tribunal of the Christ.

> This is a sober admonishment to all Christians. Why do we belittle our brothers (those who are also in Christ along with us). We often allow little things to create major divisions and even sever relationships, yet these people are our brothers. Other times we error on the other side and continue in fellowship with those who are not the Lord's, simply because they are likable individuals. This ought not to be – we must not *judge* or *belittle our <u>brothers</u>*, as we will all equally be judged by Christ.

11 For it is written, As I live, saith the Lord, every knee shall bow to me, and every tongue shall confess to God.

12 So then each one of us shall give account of himself to God.

> There is much to be said against individualism in one sense of the word, but in this matter of our personal life before Christ, it is indeed an individual matter. Regarding the things that are not sin, of how we live out our calling before the Lord, of that we will be judged by a more righteous judge than ourselves, Jesus Christ.

13 Let us, therefore, not judge one another any more, but judge this rather: that no man put a stumblingblock or an occasion to fall in *his* brother's way.

> How many of us must admit that we have put stumblingblocks in front of our brothers at some point in our lives. How careful we must be in our conversation. Not fearful, but careful. The only way to avoid being a stumblingblock is to first of all love God with all our heart, soul, mind, and strength, and to love our neighbor as ourselves (Luke 10:27-28). We must take captive every thought (2 Corinthians 10:5), and follow the Lord as He leads us. He will not leave without wisdom those who ask (James 1:5).

14 I know and trust in the Lord Jesus that for his sake there is nothing unclean, but to him that esteems any thing to be unclean, to him *it is* unclean.

> Paul is clearly talking about food here (see v. 15).

Some take this scripture and say Christians can do whatever they want, using it for an excuse to watch secular movies, indulge in sports and other pleasure, and in general live just like the heathen. That is clearly not what Paul is talking about here, and other scripture, including what we've read so far, clearly confirms this. This is not to say that all secular movies are to be avoided and that one cannot get involved in sports, but in a general sense, these things ought not to have place in a Christian's life, if we truly love the Lord and live for Him.

15 But if thy brother is grieved because of *thy* food, now thou dost not walk in charity. Do not destroy him with thy food, for whom Christ died.

16 Let not then your good be evil spoken of;

17 for the kingdom of God is not food and drink, but righteousness and peace and joy in the Holy Spirit.

We must be care less about our own preferences of *food and drink* than we care about *righteousness and peace and joy in the Holy Spirit*. If our liberties cause others to stumble, how is that a good thing? We could say "that's their problem," but it really is our problem, and we are not where we ought to be if we cause our *brother to be grieved*.

18 For he that in these things serves the Christ *is* well pleasing unto God and approved of men.

19 Let us, therefore, follow after the things which make for peace and the edification of each one to the others.

> If we care more for our brothers' spiritual wellbeing than for our own appetites, and this includes our weaker brothers, then we are in reality serving the Lord Jesus Christ Himself (v. 18).

20 Because of food, do not destroy the work of God. All things indeed *are* clean, but *it is* evil for that man who eats with offense.

21 *It is* good neither to eat flesh nor to drink wine nor *do any thing* by which thy brother stumbles or is offended or is sick.

> Paul not only preaches this, he also lived it, being all things to all men, for the sake of their salvation. *To the weak I became as weak, that I might gain the weak; I am made all things to everyone, that I might by all means save some* (1 Corinthians 9:22). This ought also to be our aim – to win all to Christ, being willing to forsake all our personal desires, for the winning of others to Christ.

22 Thou hast faith; have *it* to thyself before God. Blessed *is* he that does not condemn himself with that thing which he allows.

23 And he that makes a difference is condemned if he eats, because *he* does not *eat* by faith; and whatsoever *is* not out of faith is sin.

> *Whatsoever is not out of faith is sin.* What a powerful, sobering statement. How freely we go about this business called life, and how few consider those they are influencing by their good or bad behavior.

Romans 15

1 ¶ We then that are stronger ought to bear the infirmities of the weak, and not please ourselves.

> We generally think weaker ones should "grow up," and while that sometimes is true, Paul is here clearly admonishing us to *bear the infirmities of the weak*. This certainly does not mean we should sanction sin. Sin is not defined as a "weakness" or a "struggle" in scripture. Instead, Paul is talking about those who are weak in <u>faith</u>. It should be as natural to us to bear the *infirmities of the weak* in faith as it would be to bear the infirmities of those with mental and physical weaknesses.

2 Let each one of us please *his* neighbour in *that which is* good, unto edification.

3 For the Christ did not please himself; but, as it is written, The reproaches of those that reproached thee fell on me.

Jesus Christ is our prime example when it comes to not pleasing ourselves (v. 3). Not only did the Lord not please Himself, He also took on the reproaches of those who reproached God Himself. Can you bear the reproaches of your brothers and sisters in Christ, for the sake of Christ?

4 For the things that were written beforehand were written for our instruction that we, through patient *endurance* and through the comfort of the scriptures, might have hope.

All scripture is given to us for our benefit, so that we might have *hope.* Imagine for a moment if we didn't have the scriptures. We'd likely lose all hope. But praise God, He knew our need and made sure that many examples of faith and endurance have been recorded for our benefit. We know that *he that shall endure unto the end, the same shall be saved* (Matthew 24:13), and with all of scripture to show us how and to encourage us, we have plenty of examples to help us along the way.

5 ¶ Now the God of patience and consolation grant you to be unanimous among yourselves according to Christ Jesus,

6 that ye may with one accord *and* one mouth glorify the God and Father of our Lord Jesus Christ.

7 ¶ Therefore bear one another, as the Christ also bore us, to the glory of God.

Genuine unity does not come as a result of

compromising, but as a result of the stronger brothers *bearing the infirmities of the weak* (v. 1), *as the Christ also bore us, to the glory of God*. For all our brothers and sisters in Christ, regardless of their measure of faith (Romans 12:3, 6), are to love one another and praise God with *one mouth*.

8 Now I say that Christ Jesus, was *a* minister of the circumcision, by the truth of God, to confirm the promises *made* unto the fathers;

> Jesus Christ was a Jew, and fulfilled the promises and prophecy of scripture in great detail. Jesus said *I am not sent but unto the lost sheep of the house of Israel* (Matthew 15:24), and while He did minister to some Gentiles, it was not His chief aim, and in fact, He seemed to resist having anything to do with Gentiles. This was necessary in order to fulfill the promises that were made to the Jewish fathers of faith.

9 but that the Gentiles glorify God by mercy; as it is written, For this cause I will confess thee among the Gentiles and sing unto thy name.

10 And again he says, Rejoice, ye Gentiles, with his people.

11 And again, Praise the Lord, all ye Gentiles; and magnify him, all the peoples.

12 And again, Isaiah says, There shall be a root of Jesse and he that shall rise to reign over the Gentiles; in him the Gentiles shall wait *for salvation*.

The Gentiles waited for salvation, and *glorify God by mercy* (v. 9), meaning that we Gentiles have no promise of salvation, but are truly saved only because God was merciful and reached out above and beyond to save us. Paul was especially sent to the Gentiles, and the Jews were also shown that salvation was for the Gentiles (Acts 10). This didn't happen, however, until Jesus had completely fulfilled all the promises.

13 ¶ And believing, the God of hope fills you with all joy and peace that ye may abound in hope by the virtue of the Holy Spirit.

> Are you *filled with joy and peace*? Are you *abounding in hope by the virtue of the Holy Spirit*? Society, and even many Christians, go to endless measures to attempt to achieve joy and peace, but the source is *the God of hope*, and nothing else.

14 ¶ But I am convinced regarding you, my brethren, that even without my exhortation ye are full of charity, full of all knowledge, so as to be able to admonish one another.

15 Nevertheless I have written, brethren, in part boldly, as admonishing you by the grace that is given *to* me of God,

16 being the minister of Jesus Christ, to the Gentiles, ministering the gospel of God, that the offering of the Gentiles might be well pleasing, sanctified by the Holy Spirit.

> To what great length Paul goes in order to admonish

those under his care, to make sure they are *full of charity, knowledge, and able to admonish one another.* How much more edifying our churches would be today if pastors were able to lead their congregations to *the God of hope* as well as teach them how to *admonish one another* in love and truth, rather than trying to be hope for the congregation, and doing all the admonishing himself. We'd experience rapid growth in our churches if this were done, but first it is necessary to teach the full counsel of God, as Paul already has been doing leading up to this.

17 ¶ Therefore I have something to boast of in Christ Jesus, with regard to God.

18 For I will not dare to speak of any of those things which Christ has not wrought by me, unto the obedience of the Gentiles, with word and with deed,

19 with power of signs and wonders, in virtue of the Spirit of God; so that from Jerusalem and round about unto Illyricum, I have filled the entire *area* with the gospel of the Christ.

> Albert Barnes wrote that the area in which Paul was ministering is as follows: "Taking Jerusalem as a center, Paul preached not only in Damascus and Arabia, but in Syria, in Asia Minor, in all Greece, in the Grecian Islands, and in Thessaly and Macedonia. This comprehended no small part of the then known world; "all" of which had heard the gospel by the labors of one indefatigable man."

Paul indeed had *something to boast of in Christ Jesus, with regard to God.* Was he boasting for the sake of boasting or did he do this for his own gain? Not at all. No sane, natural man would give up everything comfortable and enjoyable, in order to preach the gospel so extensively, in the face of intense persecution. True ministers of the gospel do what they do solely out of obedience to Christ.

20 And in this manner I preached this gospel, not where Christ had been named *previously*, not to build upon a foundation belonging to another,

21 but, as it is written, To whom he was not spoken of, they shall see, and those that have not heard shall understand.

You and I may not have the opportunity to go where Christ has not yet been preached. Yet we are responsible *not to build upon a foundation belonging to another*. How we go, and to whom we go, must be directed by the Lord. If we truly follow Him, those who hear, *shall understand.*

22 ¶ For which reason I have even been hindered many times from coming to you.

Paul was hindered from coming to the Romans not because he was busy raising funds, working, or golfing, but because he was busy *preaching this gospel*! How easily we settle into life and how often the gospel we preach is corrupted with man's ideas, programs, and methodology. Paul truly went in the power of the Holy Spirit, unwilling to compromise in anything, and it is imperative that we follow his example.

23 But now having more place in these parts and having a great desire these many years to come unto you,

24 when I leave for Spain, I will come unto you; for I trust to see you on my journey and to be taken there by you, if first I may enjoy your company.

25 But now I go unto Jerusalem to minister unto the saints.

> Can you imagine having Paul come minister to you? Perhaps you are already a saint (v. 25), but to have someone who genuinely loves and uncompromisingly serves Christ minister to us is such a sweet blessing, as even saints need to be ministered unto. And yes, we also are called to minister to each other just as Paul was ministering to the saints.

26 For it has pleased those of Macedonia and Achaia to make a certain contribution for the poor saints who are in Jerusalem.

27 It has pleased them verily, and they are their debtors. For if the Gentiles have been made partakers of their spiritual things, they should also minister unto them in carnal things.

> If we receive spiritual blessing from someone, we should be willing to share our earthly things with them. Not unwillingly, but out of realizing that we

are indebted to them. Not to make them rich, but to bless them in return and to take care of their needs as they took care of ours.

28 So that, when I have concluded this and have delivered unto them this fruit, I will come by you unto Spain.

Paul thought this was important enough that he was willing to *deliver unto them this fruit.* Not that he only cared to delivery earthly goods and he certainly also ministered spiritual food to the saints in Jerusalem, but he did made time for the earthly ministry too.

29 For I know that when I come to you, I shall come in the fullness of the blessing of the gospel of the Christ.

Not a partial blessing of the gospel of Christ, but *in the fulness of the blessing of the gospel of the Christ.* This once again shows the uncompromising heart of Paul, as our heart also must be. As we do this, we will also go with *the fulness of the blessing of the gospel of the Christ.*

30 ¶ But I beseech you, brethren, by our Lord Jesus Christ, and by the charity of the Spirit, that ye help me with prayers to God for me,

31 that I may be delivered from the disobedient in Judaea and that the offering of my service to the saints in Jerusalem may be accepted,

32 that I may come unto you with joy by the will of God and may be refreshed together with you.

Paul was very specific with his prayer request, and how unselfish were his requests! How often do we pray that *the offering of my service* may be accepted? And this is to be our *offering* as well, that of *service to the saints*. Let's refresh and *be refreshed together* in Christ.

33 Now the God of peace *be* with you all. Amen.

Romans 16

1 ¶ I commend unto you Phebe our sister, who is a servant of the *congregation*[1] which is at Cenchrea,

2 that ye receive her in the Lord as a worthy saint, and that ye assist her in whatever thing in which she has need of you, for she has been a helper of many and of myself also.

> This balances out 2 Corinthians 3:1-5, where Paul makes it clear that he isn't looking for *letters of commendation* from men. In this chapter we just started, Paul will point out several notable brothers and sisters in Christ who have helped him and who he wishes others to recognize as helpful in the ministry of Christ. It's one thing to go around calling attention to ourselves, and quite another to make the church aware of individuals who are already worthy *fellow workers in Christ Jesus.*

---

1   Gr. ekklesia – called out ones

3 Greet Priscilla and Aquila, my fellow workers in Christ Jesus

4 (who have for my life laid down their own necks; unto whom not only I give thanks, but also all the *congregations*[2] of the Gentiles);

> How rare it is that men put their own life on the line for the sake of Christ. Even missionaries today when at risk of their own life will often refrain from speaking boldly for the sake of Christ. It is true that we need to be led by the Holy Spirit in these things and that may sometimes mean being quiet, but let's also be bold as much as we ought to for the sake of Christ, helping our brothers and sisters in Christ to the point of risking our *own necks*.

5 likewise *greet* the *congregation*[3] in their house. Salute my wellbeloved Epaenetus, who is the firstfruits of Achaia in Christ.

6 Greet Mary, who has laboured much with us.

> In this day when there is much talk about equality of men and women, and women going beyond what is their natural roles in order to become leaders of businesses, nations, and even churches, it is yet important to note that women have appropriate, biblical opportunity to *labor much* with the Lord's workers. There is so much that women can do which doesn't venture into men's roles as defined by scripture, that women if they fulfilled all they are given

---

2   Gr. ekklesia – called out ones
3   Gr. ekklesia – called out ones

opportunity to do, wouldn't have time to seek to also fulfill men's roles, neither would they feel the need to do so. Both men and women will truly be fulfilled in their ministry if we simply apply what the Lord says regarding these matters.

7 Salute Andronicus and Junia, my kinsmen *and my fellowprisoners*, who are of note among the apostles, who also were in Christ before me.

8 Greet Amplias, my beloved in the Lord.

9 Salute Urbane, our helper in Christ, and Stachys, my beloved.

10 Salute Apelles, approved in Christ. Salute those who are of Aristobulus' *household*.

11 Salute Herodion, my kinsman. Greet those that are of the *household* of Narcissus who are in the Lord.

12 Salute Tryphena and Tryphosa, who labour in the Lord. Salute the beloved Persis, who laboured much in the Lord.

13 Salute Rufus, chosen in the Lord, and his mother and mine.

14 Salute Asyncritus, Phlegon, Hermas, Patrobas, Hermes, and the brethren who are with them.

15 Salute Philologus and Julia, Nereus and his sister, and Olympas, and all the saints who are with them.

16 Salute one another with a holy kiss. All the *congregations*[4] of Christ salute you.

> By *holy kiss*, Paul is making it clear that this is not an inappropriate kiss, but one of genuine love. Should we greet one another with a holy kiss today? It depends on if it is appropriate. In some cultures, it is. In other cultures and situations, it is inappropriate. Be wise and don't go beyond what is prudent.

17 ¶ And I beseech you, brethren, mark those who cause dissensions and offences outside of the doctrine which ye have learned, and avoid them.

> Today, we have so many divisions and heresies, and we must avoid incorrect doctrine and those who teach them, sticking rather with what is true, which we learn by reading and believing the Bible. We must be willing to forsake our own opinions and even what we've been taught, instead allowing the Lord to lead is in all truth. This is different than bearing with individuals who are weak in faith – this is dealing with false teachers.

18 For they that are such do not serve our Lord Jesus Christ, but their own belly and by smooth words and blessings deceive the hearts of the simple.

> *By smooth words and blessings.* If someone abounds with flattery for you, that itself is reason to be cautious. It's very likely that he really only wants something for himself, to somehow fill his *own belly*.

---

4   Gr. ekklesia – called out ones

19 For your obedience is come abroad unto all *places*. I am glad therefore on your behalf, but yet I would have you wise unto that which is good and innocent concerning evil.

> Under the guise of wanting to be prepared, some Christians spend far too much time learning about all the evil that is going on in the world. The balance should be that we are *wise unto that which is good and innocent concerning evil*.

20 And let the God of peace bruise Satan under your feet quickly. The grace of our Lord Jesus Christ *be* with you. Amen.

> Our job is to *let the God of peace bruise Satan*, and that *quickly*. Will He do that through us? It says here that Satan will be bruised by *God … under our feet*, which apparently happens as we are walking with Christ. As we follow Christ, Satan will be bruised. It's a supernatural, spiritual reality. Our focus is to be on Christ, not on Satan, and as we do that, God will Himself *bruise Satan*.

21 ¶ Timothy my fellow worker and Lucius and Jason and Sosipater, my kinsmen, salute you.

22 I, Tertius, who wrote *this* epistle, salute you in the Lord.

23 Gaius my host, and of the whole *congregation*,[5] salutes you. Erastus, the chamberlain of the city, salutes you, and Quartus, a brother.

---

5 Gr. ekklesia – called out ones

24 The grace of our Lord Jesus Christ, *be* with you all. Amen.

> To end with a blessing is appropriate. What higher blessing can we receive except the *grace of the Lord Jesus Christ*? This is not a casual ending, but a sincere blessing from Paul through Tertius, who apparently was the scribe for Paul (v. 22).

25 ¶ Now to him that is able to confirm you according to my gospel and the preaching of Jesus Christ, according to the revelation of the mystery which was concealed from times eternal

> Who other than the Lord Himself is able to confirm us, confirming that we are participants in the salvation of Christ? *For of him and by him and in him are all things* (Romans 11:36).

26 but now is made manifest, and by the writings of the prophets, by the commandment *of* God eternal, declared unto all the Gentiles, that they might *hear and* obey by faith,

27 to God, only wise, *be* glory through Jesus Christ for ever. Amen.

Amen!

Other Books to Enjoy

Following Christ, by Charles H. Spurgeon

You cannot have Christ if you will not serve Him. If you take Christ, you must take Him in all His qualities. You must not simply take Him as a Friend, but you must also take Him as your Master. If you are to become His disciple, you must also become His servant. God-forbid that anyone fights against that truth. It is certainly one of our greatest delights on earth to serve our Lord, and this is to be our joyful vocation even in heaven itself: His servants shall serve Him: and they shall see His face (Revelation 22:3-4).

Available where books are sold.

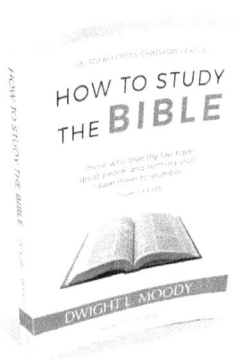

***How to Study the Bible*, by Dwight L. Moody**

This classic book by Dwight L. Moody brings to light the necessity of studying the Scriptures, presents methods which help stimulate excitement for the Scriptures, and offers tools to help you comprehend the difficult passages in the Scriptures. To live a victorious Christian life, you must read and understand what God is saying to you. Moody is a master of using stories to illustrate what he is saying, and you will be both inspired and convicted to pursue truth from the pages of God's Word.

Available where books are sold.

The Ten Commandments, by Dwight L. Moody

This book will challenge you to examine God's rules for life. God doesn't ask anything of us that is difficult or unreasonable, and this is certainly true with Jesus Christ as our strength and the Holy Spirit to guide us. This book is a challenging yet refreshing look at some of the oldest, most well-known words of God.

Available where books are sold.

Daniel, Man of God, by Dwight L. Moody

God will exalt us when the time is right. We needn't try to promote ourselves; we needn't struggle for position. Let God put us where He wants us and let us be true to God. It is better for a man to be right with God, even if he holds no great earthly position. It is honest and humble men whom God will promote, if He so desires.

This study illustrates what Daniel did, and also what Daniel didn't do, which caught the attention of God and kings alike. Few are the men in history of Daniel's caliber, even though the principles he followed can be implemented by all. Are you ready to be a truly great man, one that will cause God and men to take notice?

Available where books are sold.

The Pursuit of God, by A. W. Tozer

To have found God and still to pursue Him is a paradox of love, scorned indeed by the too-easily-satisfied religious person, but justified in happy experience by the children of the burning heart. Saint Bernard of Clairvaux stated this holy paradox in a musical four-line poem that will be instantly understood by every worshipping soul:

> *We taste Thee, O Thou Living Bread,*
> *And long to feast upon Thee still:*
> *We drink of Thee, the Fountainhead*
> *And thirst our souls from Thee to fill.*

Available where books are sold.

Pilgrim's Progress, by John Bunyan

Often disguised as something that would help him, evil accompanies Christian on his journey to the Celestial City. As you walk with him, you'll begin to identify today's many religious pitfalls. These are presented by men such as Pliable, who turns back at the Slough of Despond; and Ignorance, who believes he's a true follower of Christ when he's really only trusting in himself. Each character represented in this allegory is intentionally and profoundly accurate in its depiction of what we see all around us, and unfortunately, what we too often see in ourselves. But while Christian is injured and nearly killed, he eventually prevails to the end. So can you.

Available where books are sold.

www.ingramcontent.com/pod-product-compliance
Lightning Source LLC
Chambersburg PA
CBHW070144080526
44586CB00015B/1840